Sadlier

We Are the Church

Grade Three

Sadlier
A Division of William H. Sadlier, Inc.

Nihil Obstat
Reverend John G. Stillmank, S.T.L.
Censor Librorum

Imprimatur

✠ Most Reverend William H. Bullock
Bishop of Madison
March 6, 2003

The *Nihil Obstat* and *Imprimatur* are official declarations that a book or pamphlet is free of doctrinal or moral error. No implication is contained therein that those who have granted the *Nihil Obstat* and *Imprimatur* agree with the contents, opinions, or statements expressed.

Acknowledgments

Excerpts from the English translation of the *Catechism of the Catholic Church* for the United States of America, copyright © 1994, United States Catholic Conference, Inc.—Libreria Editrice Vaticana. English translation of the *Catechism of the Catholic Church: Modifications from the Editio Typica* copyright © 1997, United States Catholic Conference, Inc.—Libreria Editrice Vaticana. Used with permission.

Scripture excerpts are taken from the *New American Bible with Revised New Testament and Psalms*. Copyright © 1991, 1986, 1970 Confraternity of Christian Doctrine, Inc., Washington, D.C. Used with permission. All rights reserved. No part of the *New American Bible* may be reproduced by any means without permission in writing from the copyright owner.

Excerpts from the English translation of *Lectionary for Mass* © 1969, 1981, International Committee on English in the Liturgy, Inc. (ICEL); excerpts from the English translation of *Rite of Holy Week* © 1972, ICEL; excerpts from the English translation of *The Roman Missal* © 1973, ICEL; excerpts from the English translation of *Rite of Penance* © 1974, (ICEL); excerpts from the English translation of *Eucharistic Prayers for Masses of Reconciliation* © 1975, ICEL; excerpts from the English translation of *Pastoral Care of the Sick: Rites of Anointing and Viaticum* © 1982, ICEL; excerpts from the English translation of *A Book of Prayers* © 1982, ICEL. All rights reserved.

Excerpts from *Catholic Household Blessings and Prayers*, copyright © 1988, United States Catholic Conference, Inc. Washington, D.C. Used with permission. All rights reserved.

English translation of the Lord's Prayer, Glory to the Father, and the Apostles' Creed by the International Consultation on English Texts. (ICET)

From *The Collected Works of St. Teresa of Avila, Volume Two* translated by Kieran Kavanaugh and Otilio Rodriguez. Copyright © 1980 by Washington Province of Discalced Carmelites, ICS Publications, 2131 Lincoln Road, N.E., Washington, D.C. 20002–1199 U.S.A. www.icspublications.org

From *The Diary of a Young Girl, The Definitive Edition* by Anne Frank. Otto H. Frank & Mirjam Pressler, Editors, translated by Susan Massotty, copyright © 1995 by Doubleday, a division of Random House, Inc. Used by permission of Doubleday, a division of Random House, Inc.

"We Believe, We Believe in God," © 1979, North American Liturgy Resources (NALR), 5536 NE Hassalo, Portland, OR 97213. All rights reserved. Used with permission. "Lift High the Cross," words: George W. Kitchin; rev. Michael R. Newbolt. © 1974 by Hope Publishing Co., Carol Stream, IL 60188. All rights reserved. Used with permission.

"Whatsoever You Do," © 1966, 1982, Willard F. Jabusch. Administered by OCP Publications, 5536 NE Hasslo, Portland, OR 97213. All rights reserved. Used with permission. "Jesus Is with Us," © 1990, OCP Publications, 5536 NE Hassalo, Portland, OR 97213. All rights reserved. Used with permission. "We Sing Your Glory," © 1999, Bernadette Farrell. Published by OCP Publications, 5536 NE Hassalo, Portland, OR 97213. All rights reserved. Used with permission. "They'll Know We Are Christians," Peter Scholtes. © 1966, F.E.L. Publications. Assigned 1991 to the Lorenz Corporation. All rights reserved. International copyright secured. "Only a Shadow," © 1971, Carey Landry and North American Liturgy Resources (NALR), 5536 NE Hassalo, Portland, OR 97213. All rights reserved. Used with permission. "Prepare the Way," © 1991, Christopher Walker. Published by OCP Publications, 5536 NE Hassalo, Portland, OR 97213. All rights reserved. Used with permission. "Do Not Delay," © 1995, Anne Quigley. Published by OCP Publications, 5536 NE Hassalo, Portland, OR 97213. All rights reserved. Used with permission. "Jesus, We Believe in You," © 1990, Carey Landry and North American Liturgy Resources (NALR), 5536 NE Hassalo, Portland, OR 97213. All rights reserved. Used with permission. "Walking Up to Jesus," © 1993, Daughters of Charity and Christopher Walker. Published by OCP Publications, 5536 NE Hassalo, Portland, OR 97213. All rights reserved. Used with permission. "Ashes," © 1978, New Dawn Music, 5536 NE Hassalo, Portland, OR 97213. All rights reserved. Used with permission. "We Are the Church," © 1991, Christopher Walker. Published by OCP Publications, 5536 NE Hassalo, Portland, OR 97213. All rights reserved. Used with permission. "We Are the Church" was originally from "Come, Follow Me" music program, Benziger Publishing Company. "Sing a Song to the Saints," © 1991, Jack Louden. Published by OCP Publications, 5536 NE Hassalo, Portland, OR 97213. All rights reserved. Used with permission. "Glory and Praise to Our God," © 1976, Daniel L. Schutte and New Dawn Music, 5536 NE Hassalo, Portland, OR 97213. All rights reserved. Used with permission.

William H. Sadlier, Inc.
9 Pine Street
New York, NY 10005-1002

ISBN: 0-8215-5503-0
9/09 08

The Ad Hoc Committee to Oversee the Use of the Catechism,
United States Conference of Catholic Bishops,
has found this catechetical text, copyright 2004,
to be in conformity with the *Catechism of the Catholic Church.*

The Sadlier *We Believe* Program was developed by nationally recognized experts in catechesis, curriculum, and child development. These teachers of the faith and practitioners helped us to frame every lesson to be age-appropriate and appealing. In addition, a team including respected catechetical, liturgical, pastoral, and theological experts shared their insights and inspired the development of the program.

The Program is truly based on the wisdom of the community, including:

Gerard F. Baumbach, Ed.D.
Executive Vice President and Publisher

Carole M. Eipers, D.Min.
Director of Catechetics

Catechetical and Liturgical Consultants

Reverend Monsignor John F. Barry
Pastor, American Martyrs Parish
Manhattan Beach, CA

Sister Linda Gaupin, CDP, Ph.D.
Director of Religious Education
Diocese of Orlando

Mary Jo Tully
Chancellor, Archdiocese of Portland

Reverend Monsignor John M. Unger
Assoc. Superintendent for Religious Education
Archdiocese of St. Louis

Curriculum and Child Development Consultants

Brother Robert R. Bimonte, FSC
Former Superintendent of Catholic Education
Diocese of Buffalo

Gini Shimabukuro, Ed.D.
Associate Director/Associate Professor
Institute for Catholic Educational Leadership
School of Education, University of
San Francisco

Catholic Social Teaching Consultants

John Carr
Secretary, Department of Social Development
and World Peace, USCCB

Joan Rosenhauer
Coordinator, Special Projects
Department of Social Development and
World Peace, USCCB

Inculturation Consultants

Reverend Allan Figueroa Deck, SJ, Ph.D.
Executive Director, Loyola Institute for
Spirituality, Orange, CA

Kirk Gaddy
Principal, St. Katharine School
Baltimore, MD

Reverend Nguyễn Việt Hưng
Vietnamese Catechetical Committee

Dulce M. Jiménez-Abreu
Director of Spanish Programs
William H. Sadlier, Inc.

Contents

UNIT 3 The Church Leads Us in Worship 129

WE BELIEVE

The *We Believe* program will help us to

learn
   celebrate
      share and **live our Catholic faith.**

Throughout the year we will hear about many saints and holy people.

Saint Andrew Nam-Thuong

Saint Augustine

Saint Charles Lwanga

Saint Clare of Assisi

Saint Dominic Savio

Saint Elizabeth of Hungary

Saint Felicity

Saint Francis of Assisi

Saint Joan of Arc

Saint John the Apostle

Blessed Pope John XXIII

Pope John Paul II

Saint Katharine Drexel

Saint Louise de Marillac

Saint Lucy

Saint Martin de Porres

Martyrs of El Salvador—
   Sisters Ita Ford, Maura Clarke, and Dorothy Kazel; Jean Donovan

Saint Nicholas

Our Lady of Guadalupe

Saint Paul

Saint Perpetua

Saint Peter Claver

Saint Stephen

Together, let us grow as a community of faith.

Welcome!

INTRODUCTORY CHAPTER

WE GATHER

✝ **Leader:** Welcome, everyone, to Grade 3
We Believe. As we begin each chapter,
we gather in prayer. We pray to God together.

Let us sing the
We Believe song!

♫ We Believe, We Believe in God

We believe in God;
We believe, we believe in Jesus;
We believe in the Spirit who gives us life.
We believe, we believe in God.

We believe in the Holy Spirit,
Who renews the face of the earth.
We believe we are part of a living Church,
And forever we will live with God.

We believe in God;
We believe, we believe in Jesus;
We believe in the Spirit who gives us life.
We believe, we believe in God.

When we see **We Gather** we also come together as a class.

 means it's time to

think about
talk about
write about
draw about
act out

Life

at home
in our neighborhood
at school
in our parish
in our world

Talk about your life right now. What groups do you belong to?

What does belonging to these groups tell other people about you?

Each day we learn more about God.

WE BELIEVE

We learn about

- the Blessed Trinity: God the Father, God the Son, and God the Holy Spirit
- Jesus, the Son of God who became one of us
- the Church and its history and teachings
- the Mass and the sacraments
- our call to discipleship.

We find out about the different ways Catholics live their faith and celebrate God's love.

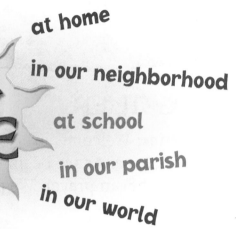

When we see **We Believe** we learn more about our Catholic faith.

Whenever we see ✝ we make the sign of the cross. We pray and begin our day's lesson.

Each of these signs points out something special that we are going to do.

📖 is an open Bible. When we see it or something like this (John 17:20–21), we hear the word of God. We hear about God and his people. We hear about Jesus and the Holy Spirit.

means we have an activity. We might

talk   write   act
  draw
      sing
work together   imagine

There are all kinds of activities! We might see 🏃 in any part of our day's lesson. Be on the lookout!

As Catholics...

Each week, we discover something special about our faith in the **As Catholics** box. Don't forget to read it!

🎵 means it is time to sing or listen to music! We sing songs we know, make up our own songs, and sing along with those in our *We Believe* music program.

Key Words means it is time to review the important words we have learned in the day's lesson.

WE RESPOND

We can respond by

- thinking about ways our faith affects the things we say and do

- sharing our thoughts and feelings

- praying to God.

Then in our homes, neighborhood, school, parish, and world, we can say and do the things that show love for God and others.

When we see **We Respond** we think about and act on what we have learned about God and our Catholic faith.

In this space, draw yourself as a *We Believe* third grader.

We are so happy you are with us!

Review

Here we answer questions about what we have learned in this chapter.

Reflect & Pray

We take a few moments to think about our faith and to pray.

Key Words

We review each of the Key Words.

Review

Grade 3
Chapter 1

Circle the letter beside the correct answer.

1. The _____ is the three Persons in one God.

   a. Incarnation   b. Bible   c. Blessed Trinity

2. The _____ is the truth that the Son of God became man.

   a. Incarnation   b. Bible   c. Blessed Trinity

3. The name Jesus means "_____."

   a. God gives   b. God loves   c. God saves

4. "One who is sent" is _____.

   a. an apostle   b. a disciple   c. a follower

Complete this sentence.

5. When Jesus was growing up in his family,

   _____

   _____

   _____

ASSESSMENT Choose one news story that tells about people in need. Then, on a large piece of paper or poster board, draw how you can help make things better in your home and school by living as Jesus did.

24

We Respond in Faith

Reflect & Pray

Jesus is divine and human. He teaches us about God's love and mercy. He shows us how to live as his faithful followers. Complete the prayer in your own words.

Jesus, I want to follow your example. Jesus, help me to

_____

_____

_____

Key Words

Blessed Trinity (p. 250)
Incarnation (p. 251)
prophet (p. 253)
repent (p. 253)
public ministry (p. 253)
disciples (p. 251)
apostle (p. 250)

Remember

- God the Son became one of us.
- Jesus grew up in Nazareth.
- Jesus begins his work.
- Jesus shows us how to live as his followers.

OUR CATHOLIC LIFE

Holy Childhood Association

The Holy Childhood Association invites children to help one another. One way that children can help one another is by collecting money for needy families all over the world. Adult members of the Holy Childhood Association tell children how families in other countries live. They show children how their money helps other children's families all over the world.

Remember

We recall the four main faith statements of the chapter.

ASSESSMENT We do a chapter activity that will show that we have discovered more about our Catholic faith.

OUR CATHOLIC LIFE

Here we read an interesting story about the ways people make the world better by living out their Catholic faith.

SHARING FAITH
with My Family

INTRODUCTORY CHAPTER

At the end of each chapter you'll bring a page like this home to share with your family.

Sharing What I Learned

Talk about
WE GATHER
WE BELIEVE   **WE RESPOND**
with your family.

A Family Prayer

(Lead your family in prayer.)

People who love us make love grow.
Thank you, God, for our family.

People who love us make love grow.
Thank you, God, for all the friends
of our family.

Most of all, thank
you, God,
for loving us!

We Believe
Family Contract

As a **We Believe** family,
this year we promise to

_____

_____

Names

_____

_____

_____

WE ARE THE CHURCH

Look here for connections to the Web and to the Catechism.

Visit Sadlier's

www.WeBelieveweb.com

Connect to the Catechism
References are given here to connect to the
Catechism of the Catholic Church.

Jesus Gives Us the Church

UNIT 1

SHARING FAITH as a Family

Belonging to a Family of Faith

What happens when a new person joins a family? A new-born baby, an adopted child, the spouse of a son or daughter—each one is *initiated* in some way. This entails sharing the family's story, including a "Who's Who" and how each person is related to the other. New members also enter the family by participating in its celebrations and learning its rules. In the best-case scenario, this process is one of *welcoming* and establishes a sense of belonging.

This is not unlike what happens in the sacrament of Baptism. Rather than expecting a newly baptized infant or adult to instantly know everything about the Catholic community, he or she is initiated through taking part in its rituals, understanding its symbols, and learning its story.

Your child will be learning more this year about what it means to follow Jesus and to belong to the Church. Just as you teach your child what it means to be part of your family, so you can help her or him take an active part in the Church. Participate in the life of the parish, talk to your child about your faith, and tell stories about Jesus. All of these things will guide your child towards taking his or her place as a precious part of the Body of Christ.

A Meditation on Holiness

As your child learns about the early Church in this unit, he or she will realize that we are all called to holiness by our membership in the Church. Try to schedule a few moments to be by yourself. We know this might not be easy to do. Close the door. Put on some soothing music.

Breathe very deeply, in and out, three times as you think to yourself: **Re** (inhale) **lax** (exhale). Feel your head drop as you count backwards from ten to zero. Now stay there for a moment of relaxation.

From the Catechism

"'The Christian family . . . can and should be called a *domestic church*.' It is a community of faith, hope, and charity."
(*Catechism of the Catholic Church*, 2204)

What Your Child Will Learn in Unit 1

One of the major emphases of Unit 1 concerns the ways that Jesus teaches us about God's love. The children will see how Jesus teaches about the Kingdom of God and shows us a God of mercy. The children will be introduced to the meaning of life everlasting. This is followed by an examination of the Church's beginnings. The children will see the early followers of Jesus share the good news with people throughout the world. They will become aware of followers who stood up for their faith under the most trying of circumstances. Lastly, the children will learn that we are all called to holiness—each in our own way.

Plan & Preview

▶ You might create a stage backdrop for all the figures collected in this unit. Help your child to look at pictures of the Holy Land. Obtain a shoebox lid or comparable stiff cardboard that the family can use to draw a scene. The figures can then be placed in front of the "stage" setting. Props such as rocks and bushes can be made from sponges and papier-mâché. Your creativity is needed!

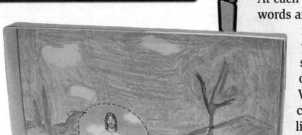

Quietly, in your mind, say the words,

Holy, holy, holy Lord,

(pause)

God of power and might,

(pause)

heaven and earth are full of your glory.

(pause)

Hosanna in the highest.

At each pause reflect on what the words are saying to you right now. What images do you see? How do you see yourself as a person of holiness today? Visualize this as you count from one to five, lifting your head up and opening your eyes.

God Sends Us His Own Son

WE GATHER

✝ **Leader:** Let us be very still and listen to this story of God's invitation to Mary to become the mother of Jesus:

📖 Luke 1:26–35

In the sixth month, the angel Gabriel was sent to Mary. The angel told Mary that she would have a son and said to her, "You shall name him Jesus." (Luke 1:31) This child will be the Son of God.

All: Loving Father, thank you for the gift of your Son, Jesus. Thank you for choosing Mary to be his mother.

Leader: Let us pray.

Side 1: Jesus is the Son of God, alleluia.

Side 2: Jesus is the son of Mary, alleluia.

Side 1: He has come to save us all, alleluia.

Side 2: He has come to save us all, alleluia.

☀ Who is someone special in your life? How do you show that this person is important to you?

WE BELIEVE

God the Son became one of us.

We believe in the Blessed Trinity. The **Blessed Trinity** is the three Persons in one God: God the Father, God the Son, and God the Holy Spirit. God the Father wants us to know his love. So he sent his only Son to be with us. God the Son, the second Person of the Blessed Trinity, became man. This truth is called the **Incarnation**.

God chose Mary to be the mother of his Son and Joseph to be his Son's foster father. The Son of God was named Jesus. *Jesus* means "God saves."

Jesus is truly the Son of God. Jesus is divine. *Divine* is a word we use to describe God. Jesus is truly the son of Mary. Jesus is human. He is like us in all things except this: He is without sin.

How did God the Father show us his great love?

Jesus grew up in Nazareth.

Jesus grew up in the town of Nazareth in Galilee. He was a Jew. During Jesus' time, mothers like Mary would teach their children how to pray. They would tell them wonderful stories of their ancestors, the Jewish people who lived before them.

Key Words

Blessed Trinity
(p. 250)

Incarnation
(p. 251)

Sons learned what their fathers did for a living. Joseph was a carpenter. Jesus learned from Joseph how to work with wood and build things. So in the Bible Jesus is called "the carpenter's son." (Matthew 13:55)

Luke 2:41–51

When Jesus was twelve years old, he went to Jerusalem to celebrate a Jewish feast with Mary, Joseph, and their relatives. After the celebration "the boy Jesus remained behind in Jerusalem, but his parents did not know it." (Luke 2:43)

Mary and Joseph searched everywhere for Jesus. They did not know that he was in the Temple talking with some teachers. Everyone was amazed at the questions Jesus asked. When Mary and Joseph found Jesus, they were surprised, too. They wanted him to return to Nazareth. Jesus obeyed and went with them.

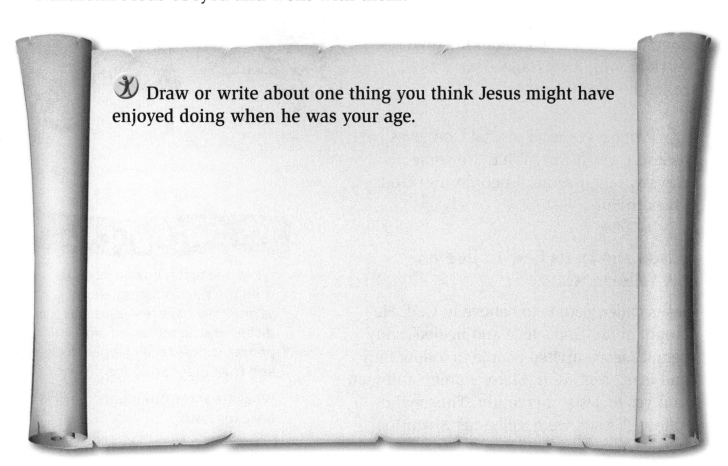

Draw or write about one thing you think Jesus might have enjoyed doing when he was your age.

Jesus begins his work.

Jesus had a cousin named John. John was a prophet. A **prophet** is someone called by God to speak to the people.

John prepared the people for Jesus. He told them, "Repent, for the kingdom of heaven is at hand."(Matthew 3:2). **Repent** means to turn away from sin and to ask God for help to live a good life.

Many people were baptized by John. This washing with water was a sign of their turning away from sin and their turning to God.

Even though Jesus was without sin, he went to John to be baptized. As Jesus came out of the water, God the Holy Spirit came upon him like a dove. A voice was heard saying, "This is my beloved Son, with whom I am well pleased." (Matthew 3:17)

Soon after this Jesus began his own work among the people. This was called his **public ministry**.

 Prophets remind us that God loves us and cares for us. What are some ways you can remind people that God loves them?

Jesus shows us how to live as his followers.

Jesus called people to believe in God. He taught about God's love and healed many people. Jesus invited people to follow him and learn from him. Many women and men said yes to Jesus' invitation. Those who followed Jesus were called his **disciples**.

As Catholics...

When the first followers of Jesus used the title *Lord*, they were saying they believed Jesus was divine. By calling Jesus *Lord* people showed their respect for and trust in Jesus' divine power.

What are some other titles we have for Jesus?

In his ministry, Jesus tried to reach out to those who were ignored by others. He healed the sick and fed the hungry. He spent time with the poor and lonely. Jesus showed us how to be his disciples by the way he lived.

Jesus showed his love for God his Father by praying often. Once Jesus went by himself to a mountain to pray. He spent the whole night there in prayer. The next day he called his disciples together and chose twelve men to be his apostles. The word **apostle** means "one who is sent."

Jesus' apostles shared in his life and his work in a special way. They traveled with Jesus and became his close friends. They helped him teach and spread the message of God's love.

WE RESPOND

Use the computer screen below to design a Web page. Use words and drawings to show people from all over the world some ways to follow Jesus.

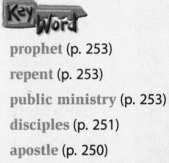

Key Word

prophet (p. 253)

repent (p. 253)

public ministry (p. 253)

disciples (p. 251)

apostle (p. 250)

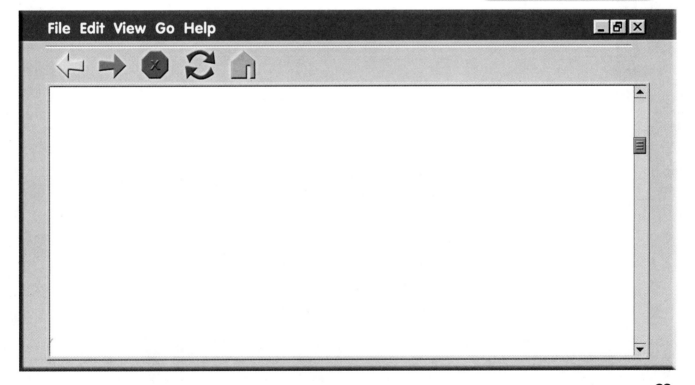

File Edit View Go Help

Review

Grade 3
Chapter 1

Circle the letter beside the correct answer.

1. The _____ is the three Persons in one God.

   a. Incarnation   **b.** Bible   **c.** Blessed Trinity

2. The _____ is the truth that the Son of God became man.

   a. Incarnation   **b.** Bible   **c.** Blessed Trinity

3. The name Jesus means "_____."

   a. God gives   **b.** God loves   **c.** God saves

4. "One who is sent" is _____.

   a. an apostle   **b.** a disciple   **c.** a follower

Complete this sentence.

5. When Jesus was growing up in his family, _____

   _____

   _____

   _____

   _____

ASSESSMENT

Choose one news story that tells about people in need. Then, on a large piece of paper or poster board, draw how you can help make things better in your home and school by living as Jesus did.

We Respond in Faith

Reflect & Pray

Jesus is divine and human. He teaches us about God's love and mercy. He shows us how to live as his faithful followers. Complete the prayer in your own words.

Jesus, I want to follow your example. Jesus, help me to

_____

_____

_____

Key Words

Blessed Trinity (p. 250)
Incarnation (p. 251)
prophet (p. 253)
repent (p. 253)
public ministry (p. 253)
disciples (p. 251)
apostle (p. 250)

Remember

- God the Son became one of us.
- Jesus grew up in Nazareth.
- Jesus begins his work.
- Jesus shows us how to live as his followers.

OUR CATHOLIC LIFE

Holy Childhood Association

The Holy Childhood Association invites children to help one another. One way that children can help one another is by collecting money for needy families all over the world. Adult members of the Holy Childhood Association tell children how families in other countries live. They show children how their money helps other children's families all over the world.

SHARING FAITH
with My Family

Sharing What I Learned

Look at the pictures below. Use each picture to tell your family what you learned in this chapter.

Family Prayer

Lead your family in this prayer.

God, our Father, we thank you for this day. Thank you for sending us your Son, Jesus, to save us and show us how to live.

Amen.

The Story of the Church

Cut out this figure of Jesus. Glue it to a piece of cardboard or stiff paper. Fold and stand. Talk with your family about Jesus and how he lived his life.

Fold

Fold

Visit Sadlier's

www.WeBelieveweb.com

Connect to the Catechism
For adult background and reflection, see paragraphs 460, 533, 517, and 561.

Jesus Teaches Us About God's Love

WE GATHER

✝ **Leader:** Let us gather together to pray.

🎵 **Lift High the Cross**

All: Lift high the cross,
the love of Christ proclaim
Till all the world adore his sacred name.

Leader: The same Lord is Lord
of all, giving to all who call upon him.
For "everyone who calls on the name of
the Lord will be saved." (Roman 10:13)

All: Lift high the cross,
the love of Christ proclaim
Till all the world adore his sacred name.

☀ How can you show that you love
your family? How do your family
members show their love for you?

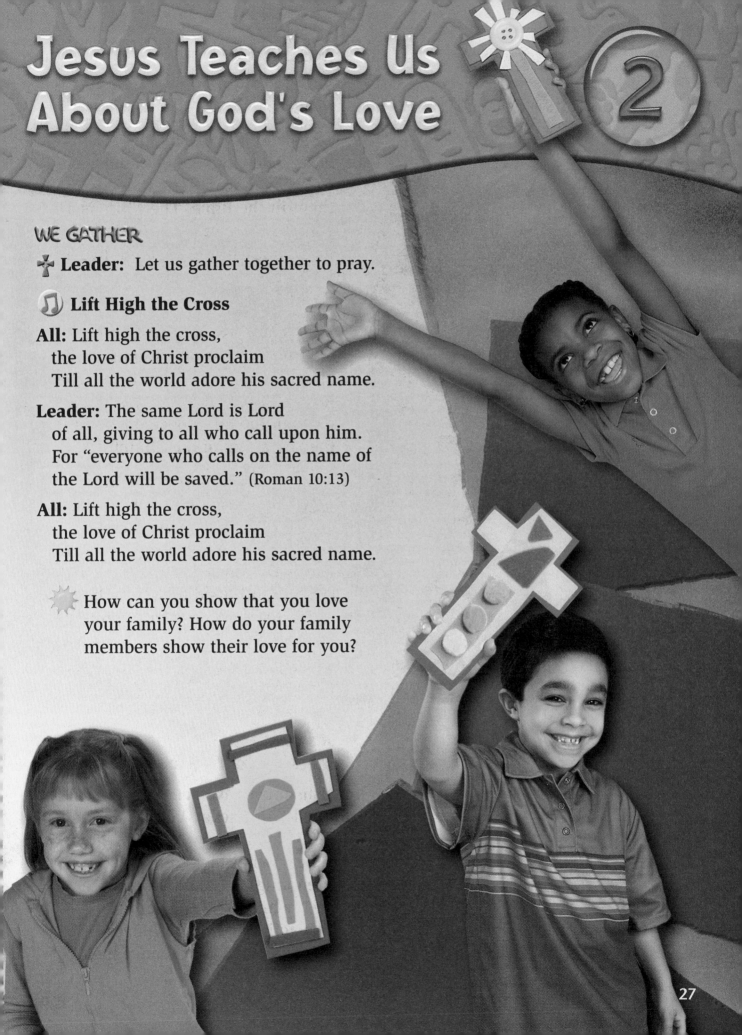

Jesus tells us how much God loves us.

Jesus taught that God loves each one of us. There are many examples of God's great love. We can read about them in the Bible. The **Bible** is a collection of books about God's love for us and about our call to live as God's people. It is also called *Scripture*.

The Bible has two parts, called *testaments*. The Old Testament is about the people of God before the time of Jesus. The New Testament is about the life of Jesus Christ and the beginning of the Church.

The human authors of the Bible were guided by God the Holy Spirit, the third Person of the Blessed Trinity. They wrote about things that God wanted to share with us. Yet the human authors did choose the words for the stories they wrote.

Talk about your favorite story about Jesus from the Bible.

Jesus teaches about the Kingdom of God.

Jesus must have been a wonderful teacher. We learn from the Bible that crowds followed him to hear what he had to say. Jesus often taught about the **Kingdom of God**, which is the power of God's love active in the world. Jesus wanted everyone to change their lives and turn to God.

Jesus taught about God's forgiveness and mercy. He taught about love and respect for others.

Jesus' greatest teaching was the way he lived. Jesus said that he "did not come to be served but to serve." (Mark 10:45) He wants us to do the same. He wants us to love one another as he loves us.

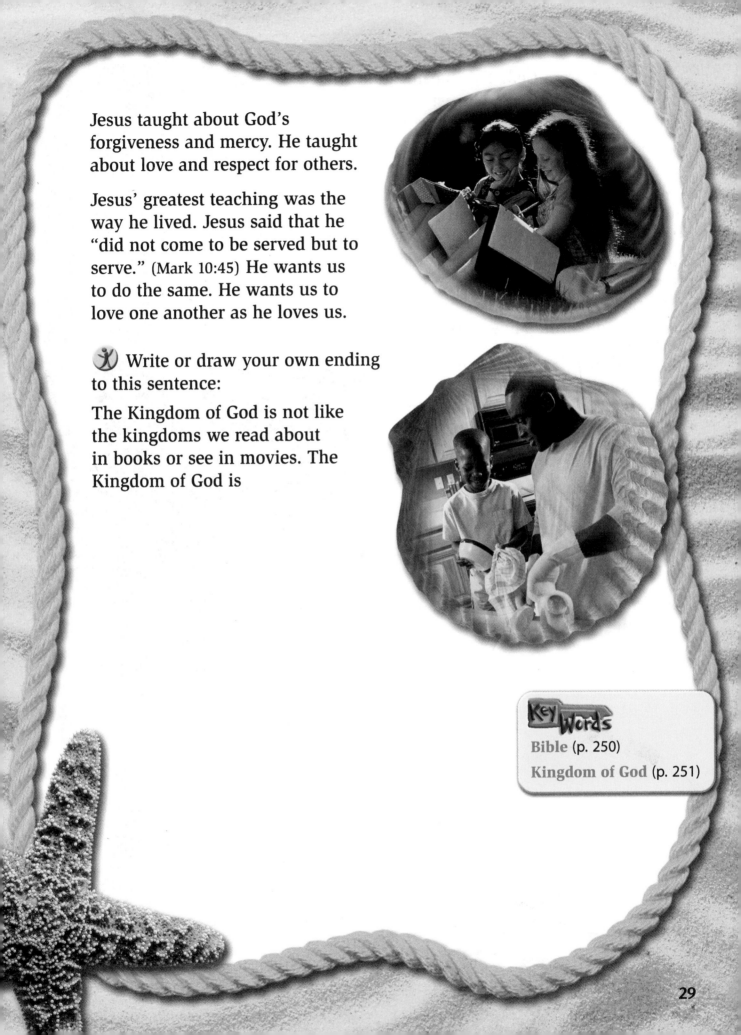 Write or draw your own ending to this sentence:

The Kingdom of God is not like the kingdoms we read about in books or see in movies. The Kingdom of God is

Key Words

Bible (p. 250)
Kingdom of God (p. 251)

Jesus teaches about the gift of faith.

Faith is a gift from God. This means that God helps us to believe and trust in him. Jesus teaches us about faith in God by his stories and his actions.

📖 Luke 17:5–6

One day Jesus was teaching. His apostles asked him to give them more faith. Jesus replied, "If you have faith the size of a mustard seed, you would say to [this] mulberry tree, 'Be uprooted and planted in the sea,' and it would obey you." (Luke 17:6)

A mustard seed is very tiny. It is about the size of the tip of a pencil. A mulberry tree is very strong. Imagine being able to make this tree lift itself into the sea!

Jesus was telling his apostles that faith is very powerful. Faith allows us to believe what we cannot see or feel or touch.

🧍 Write one way other people share their faith with you.

_____

_____

The Mulberry Tree by Vincent van Gogh

Jesus dies and rises to save us.

Jesus lived his life in such a way that people knew he loved God. Some powerful people hated Jesus because of what he did and said.

📖 Luke 23: 33–24:10

Jesus was arrested and put to death. Like a criminal, Jesus was **crucified**, nailed to a cross. Yet even as he was dying, Jesus prayed, "Father, forgive them, they know not what they do." (Luke 23:34)

Mary, the mother of Jesus, and other women disciples stayed by Jesus' cross with John the apostle. The other disciples hid because they were afraid. After Jesus died, his body was laid in a tomb.

 Luke 24: 1–12

Early Sunday morning some women returned to the tomb. They were carrying oils and spices to anoint the body of Jesus. When they reached the tomb, they saw that it was empty. The body of Jesus was not there!

Two men in dazzling garments told the women, "He is not here, but he has been raised." (Luke 24:6) The women went and told the apostles the news.

We call Jesus' being raised from the dead the Resurrection. Jesus died and rose so that all people could be saved and live with God forever.

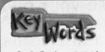

faith (p. 251)

crucified (p. 250)

Resurrection (p. 253)

WE RESPOND

Pretend you were with the women who went to the tomb. How would you have felt? What would you have done and said? Act it out.

Circle the letter beside the correct answer.

1. To believe and trust in God means to have _____.

    a. faith   **b.** fear   **c.** anger

2. The human authors of the Bible were guided by _____.

    a. Matthew   **b.** the Holy Spirit   **c.** the disciples

3. The power of God's love active in the world is the _____.

    a. Bible   **b.** Our Father   **c.** Kingdom of God

4. Jesus' being raised from the dead is called _____.

    a. the tomb   **b.** faith   **c.** the Resurrection

Use your own words to complete this sentence.

5. Faith means _____

_____

_____

_____

ASSESSMENT

Make a booklet to show ways people build up the Kingdom of God. Use magazine or newspaper pictures in your booklet.

We Respond in Faith

Reflect & Pray

All the disciples except John and the women ran away in fear when Jesus was crucified. Jesus, keep me close to you, especially when

_____

_____

_____

_____

_____

Key Words

Bible (p. 250)
Kingdom of God (p. 251)
faith (p. 251)
crucified (p. 250)
Resurrection (p. 253)

Remember

- Jesus tells us how much God loves us.
- Jesus teaches about the Kingdom of God.
- Jesus teaches about the gift of faith.
- Jesus dies and rises to save us.

OUR CATHOLIC LIFE

The Bible in Our Lives

The Bible is an important book in the lives of all Catholics. When we celebrate the sacraments, we listen to readings from this special book. As we gather with our parish community at these celebrations, we hear about God's never-ending love and kindness for his people. We learn how God wants us to live. For Catholics the Bible, the Word of God, is an important part of our faith. Each day the Word of God can come alive in our lives if we are listening to what God has to say to us.

SHARING FAITH
with My Family

Sharing What I Learned

Look at the pictures below. Use each picture to tell your family what you learned in this chapter.

Kingdom Cards

We build the Kingdom of God when we share God's love with others. Cut out the kingdom cards. Give a card to a family member. Plan a time to do the activity together. Give out as many cards as you can.

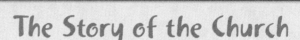

| PLAY A GAME WITH ME. | READ A BOOK WITH ME. | Read a Bible story with me. | Take a walk with me. | Go on a picnic with me. |

The Story of the Church

Cut out this picture of the women at Jesus' tomb. Glue it to a piece of cardboard or stiff paper. Fold and stand. Talk with your family about the Resurrection of Jesus.

Fold

Fold

Connect to the Catechism
For adult background and reflection, see paragraphs 104, 541, 153, and 638.

WE GATHER

Leader: Let us listen to the words of Jesus in Saint Matthew's Gospel:

Reader: "For I was hungry and you gave me food, I was thirsty and you gave me drink, a stranger and you welcomed me, naked and you clothed me, ill and you cared for me, in prison and you visited me." (Matthew 25: 35–36)

The Gospel of the Lord.

All: Praise to you, Lord Jesus Christ.

♪ Whatsoever You Do

Chorus
Whatsoever you do
to the least of my people,
that you do unto me.

When I was hungry,
you gave me to eat;
When I was thirsty,
you gave me to drink.
Now enter into the home
of my Father. (Chorus)

☀ Have you ever heard about someone who has special power? Describe what that person could do.

Jesus has power over life and death.

Jesus loved his friends. Among his best friends were Martha, Mary, and their brother Lazarus. This family lived in a town called Bethany.

 John 11:1–3, 17–44

One day Lazarus became very sick. His sisters sent a message to Jesus telling him about Lazarus. When Jesus reached Bethany, Lazarus had already died and been buried.

Martha cried to Jesus that, if he had been there, he could have cured Lazarus. Jesus said, "I am the resurrection and the life; whoever believes in me, even if he dies, will live." Martha told Jesus, "I have come to believe that you are the Messiah, the Son of God." (John 11:25, 27)

Mary, Lazarus's other sister, came to greet Jesus. She was also crying. The sisters showed Jesus where Lazarus was buried, and Jesus began to cry.

A huge rock lay across the entrance to the place where Lazarus was buried. Jesus ordered that it be taken away. Then Jesus cried out in a loud voice, "Lazarus, come out!" (John 11:43) With that, Lazarus came out.

Jesus had raised Lazarus from the dead and more people began to believe that Jesus was the Messiah, the Son of God.

Jesus is the Resurrection and the life. If he asked you, "Do you believe this?" what would you say?

36

Jesus will come again.

One day the disciples wanted Jesus to tell them when the world would end. But Jesus said, "Stay awake! For you do not know on which day your Lord will come." (Matthew 24:42)

Jesus did not mean that our bodies should never go to sleep. He meant that we should always be preparing for his coming. We do this through prayer and the things we say and do.

Jesus was born in Bethlehem. That was his first coming. Jesus will come again at the end of time, and we will see him for ourselves. Jesus' coming at the end of time will be a joyful event. It is called his **second coming**.

When Christ comes again, we will be filled with joy and happiness. We will know Jesus because we will see him. Our life with the risen Christ will go on in joy forever.

As Catholics...

Jesus' raising Lazarus from the dead was a miracle. Jesus' miracles—walking on water, calming the seas, healing the sick—went beyond human power. Each miracle was a call to believe that Jesus was sent by God to save his people. Jesus' miracles were special signs that helped people to trust and believe in God. They showed people that God's Kingdom was present in their lives.

We can "stay awake" for the second coming of Jesus Christ by living each day the way he taught us. Write one way you will "stay awake" in faith this week.

_____

_____

second coming (p. 253)

When Jesus Christ comes again, he will judge all people.

People can choose to be with God or to turn away from God. These choices will determine whether people can be with God in heaven or not. **Heaven** is life with God forever.

 Matthew 25:31–43

Jesus told his followers that at the end of time he will come in glory with all the angels. He will separate all the people into two groups, one to his right and one to his left.

Then he will tell the people on his right that they are blessed by his Father. He will say, "For I was hungry and you gave me food, I was thirsty and you gave me drink, a stranger and you welcomed me, naked and you clothed me, ill and you cared for me, in prison and you visited me." Then the people on his right will ask when they saw him like this. And he will say, "Amen, I say to you, whatever you did for one of these least brothers of mine, you did for me." (Matthew 25:35–36, 40)

Jesus will then tell those on his left to go away from him forever because they did not care for him when he was hungry, thirsty, a stranger, ill, unclothed, or in prison.

When we choose to love and care for other people, especially those who are poor or weak, we love and care for Jesus. At the last judgment we will be judged by the way we treated others. The **last judgment** is Jesus Christ coming at the end of time to judge all people.

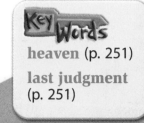

Key Words
heaven (p. 251)
last judgment (p. 251)

Name one way your parish can care for Jesus by caring for others.

_____

_____

Jesus teaches us to love others.

Jesus lived his life in perfect love of God the Father and in service to others. He is our example of holiness.

📖 Mark 12:28–32

One day, a man asked Jesus which commandment was the greatest. Jesus replied, "'You shall love the Lord your God with all your heart, with all your soul, with all your mind, and with all your strength.' The second is this: 'You shall love your neighbor as yourself.' There is no other commandment greater than these." (Mark 12:30–31)

If we love God with all of our heart and we love others as we love ourselves, we are choosing to follow Jesus. Jesus can help us make the right choices. He can give us the courage to treat others as we would like to be treated.

✞ We all have chances to be good neighbors. Act out how you can be a good neighbor in the situation shown on this page.

WE RESPOND

In a group talk about why you think Jesus told us that love is the most important thing of all.

LOVE GOD! LOVE YOUR NEIGHBOR AS YOURSELF

MILK

Review

Circle the letter beside the correct answer.

1. Jesus is the Resurrection and the _____.

   a. kingdom   **b.** crucifixion   **c.** life

2. Jesus' first coming was his birth. Jesus will come again at the _____.

   a. Last Supper   **b.** end of time   **c.** Resurrection

3. At the _____ Jesus will judge people by the way they treated others.

   a. Last Supper   **b.** Mass   **c.** last judgment

4. Life with God forever is called _____.

   a. birth   **b.** the Church   **c.** heaven

Use your own words to complete this sentence.

5. Jesus will judge us on _____

_____

_____

_____

ASSESSMENT

Look back through the chapter at Jesus' teachings. Then imagine you are a disciple traveling with Jesus. Write a letter home. Tell what you heard Jesus teach.

We Respond in Faith

Reflect & Pray

Think about the choices you make. How do they help you to follow Jesus?

Complete this prayer.

Jesus, help me

_____

_____

_____

Key Words

second coming (p. 253)
heaven (p. 251)
last judgment (p. 251)

Remember

- Jesus has power over life and death.
- Jesus will come again.
- When Jesus Christ comes again, he will judge all people.
- Jesus teaches us to love others.

OUR CATHOLIC LIFE

Care for All People

Catholics in every country reach out to those in need because we see all people as created and loved by God. The Catholic Church defends the rights of the poor and needy, the sick and the dying. We are reminded in many of the writings of Pope John Paul II to do what we can to feed the hungry, to provide homes for the homeless, and to work for peace and justice.

SHARING FAITH
with My Family

Sharing What I Learned

Look at the pictures below. Use each picture to tell your family what you learned in this chapter.

Family Prayer

(Lead your family in this prayer.)

Let us proclaim our faith.

Christ has died.
(All bow from the waist.)

Christ is risen.
(All stand.)

Christ will come again. Amen.
(All raise their hands in the air.)

Fold

Fold

The Story of the Church

Cut out this picture of Mary, Martha, and Lazarus. Glue it to a piece of cardboard or stiff paper. Fold and stand. Talk with your family about the story of Jesus and Lazarus. Keep your figure in a special place.

Visit Sadlier's
www.WeBelieve.web.com

Connect to the Catechism
For adult background and reflection, see paragraphs 547, 671, 678, and 1970.

The Church Begins

4

WE GATHER

✝ **Mary:** Come, my children, let us pray.
There will come to us this day
The Helper who will show the way.

All: Let us wait and let us pray.

Peter: Listen, listen, do you hear
A wind that is blowing strong and clear?

Andrew: A wind that seems to stir in me
No longer fear, but bravery.

James: Look, look, above each the same,
A burning fire, a glowing flame.

John: And we are filled with great desire
To spread his word like a mighty fire.

All: Spirit of Jesus, fill us all
With life and love to heed your call.
Make us brave, strong, and true.
Disciples all, we will follow you.

Alleluia. Amen.

Think back to a time
when you were afraid of
something. Who or
what gave you the
courage to overcome
your fear?

43

Pieter Coecke van Aelst
(1502–1550), *Pentecost*

WE BELIEVE

Jesus promises to send the Holy Spirit.

Jesus knew that his followers would be afraid when he had to leave them. So he promised to send them a special Helper, the Holy Spirit, who would always be with them.

📖 Matthew 28:16–20

Forty days after his Resurrection, Jesus met his apostles in Galilee. It was their last meeting with him on earth. Jesus gave his apostles a mission, or special job, to make disciples of all nations. The apostles were to baptize people everywhere in the name of God the Father, the Son, and the Holy Spirit. Jesus said, "Behold, I am with you always, until the end of the age." (Matthew 28:20)

Then Jesus ascended and returned to his Father in heaven. This event is called the Ascension. After Jesus' Ascension, his apostles returned to Jerusalem. They did not know how they would ever be able to tell the whole world about Jesus.

Mary, the mother of Jesus, also returned to Jerusalem. She prayed with the apostles and disciples as they waited for the coming of the Holy Spirit.

🏃 Think about the disciples waiting for the Holy Spirit to come. How do you think they felt?

The Holy Spirit comes to the disciples.

📖 Acts of the Apostles 2:1–41

Inside a room where they had gathered, the disciples heard a noise that sounded like a great wind. They saw what seemed to be flames of fire that spread out and touched each one of them. Suddenly, the disciples were filled with the Holy Spirit. They were changed in a wonderful way.

A large crowd was outside. The disciples came out of the room and began to speak about Jesus with great courage. Then Peter, the leader of all of the disciples, spoke to the people. He told them that God had raised Jesus from the dead. Peter told them that this Jesus who had been crucified and rose is truly the Lord, Jesus Christ.

When Peter spoke to the crowd, the people understood him in their different languages. They asked him what they should do. Peter replied, "Repent and be baptized, every one of you, in the name of Jesus Christ for the forgiveness of your sins; and you will receive the gift of the holy Spirit." (Acts of the Apostles 2:38) Many people accepted this message, and about three thousand people were baptized that day. The day on which the Holy Spirit came to the disciples is called **Pentecost**. The Holy Spirit comes to us, too. The Holy Spirit helps us to be brave followers of Jesus.

In the flame, write words that describe how the disciples were changed when the Holy Spirit came to them.

Key Words

mission (p. 252)
Ascension (p. 250)
Pentecost (p. 252)

_____

_____

_____

_____

_____

_____

_____

The Church begins on Pentecost.

On Pentecost, the disciples shared their good news about Jesus with the people gathered around them. Soon, many people were baptized and received the Holy Spirit. This was the beginning of Jesus' Church. The **Church** is the community of people who are baptized and follow Jesus Christ.

The new believers listened to the teaching of the apostles. They came together for prayer and for "the breaking of the bread" as Jesus and the apostles did at the Last Supper. (Acts of the Apostles 2:42) They shared everything they owned with one another. They cared for those among them who were poor or in need. They treated everyone with love and respect.

Soon after the coming of the Holy Spirit, the apostles and other disciples began to travel. They preached the good news of Jesus to people in other cities and countries. Communities of new believers grew everywhere. Those people who were baptized began to be called **Christians**, because they were followers of Jesus Christ.

Key Words

Church (p. 250)
Christians (p. 250)

Imagine that you are back in the time of the first Christians. You have been asked to talk to a large crowd about following Jesus. Work with a partner on a speech that would tell them what to do.

The early Church grows.

As the Church grew, people in power began to worry that too many people were becoming Christians. At that time the disciple Stephen preached about Jesus. Because of Stephen, many people became Christians. The enemies of the Church were very angry, and they had Stephen put to death.

 Acts of the Apostles 9:3–5

Saul of Tarsus was one of the men determined to stop those who believed in Jesus. One day Saul was traveling along a road and a bright light from the sky suddenly flashed around him. He fell to the ground and heard a voice saying to him, "Saul, Saul, why are you persecuting me?" Saul wanted to know who was speaking to him. Then he heard, "I am Jesus, whom you are persecuting." (Acts of the Apostles 9:4, 5)

Saul's life changed forever. Three days later he was baptized. Saul, also known as Paul, became one of the greatest followers of Jesus Christ in history.

Paul made many trips to build up Christian communities throughout the world. His preaching and example encouraged many people to believe in Christ. His work and the work of many others helped the Church to grow. People of all races, languages, and nationalities came to believe in Jesus Christ.

As Catholics...

The apostles and the first disciples told the good news of Jesus Christ to everyone. This is called *evangelization*. We are called to go out and evangelize, too. Our pope and bishops want each of us to be a part of the "new evangelization." This means that the good news of Jesus makes as much of a difference today as it did in the time of the first disciples.

WE RESPOND

We are too young to go all over the world telling people about Jesus Christ. But we can show the people in our neighborhood and parish family that we are followers of Jesus Christ. How can we do this?

_____

_____

_____

Circle the letter beside the correct answer.

1. Jesus promised to send the _____.

   a. Holy Spirit   **b.** Messiah   **c.** Father

2. Jesus told the apostles to go and _____.

   a. hide   **b.** baptize   **c.** be afraid

3. The Holy Spirit came upon the disciples on _____.

   a. the Ascension   **b.** Easter   **c.** Pentecost

4. All those who are baptized and follow Christ are called _____.

   a. teachers   **b.** enemies   **c.** Christians

Use your own words to complete the sentence.

5. The Holy Spirit is always _____

_____

_____

ASSESSMENT

Imagine you are one of the first Christians. What is life like for you? Write a paragraph or draw a cartoon strip about it.

We Respond in Faith

Reflect & Pray

We can carry out Jesus' work in the world by sharing the good news, praying, and helping others.

Think about what you can do this week at home and in school to continue Jesus' work.

Jesus, help me to carry on your work in the world. Help me to

_____

_____

Key Words

mission (p. 252)
Ascension (p. 250)
Pentecost (p. 252)
Church (p. 250)
Christians (p. 250)

Remember

- Jesus promises to send the Holy Spirit.
- The Holy Spirit comes to the disciples.
- The Church begins on Pentecost.
- The early Church grows.

OUR CATHOLIC LIFE

Good News for All

Today, the Church proclaims the good news of Jesus everywhere on earth and in every language. For example, if we travel to South America, we would hear Jesus' message in Spanish or Portuguese. In Africa, we might hear it in Swahili. Here in our own country, Mass and the other sacraments are celebrated in Mandarin, German, Polish, Spanish, and many other languages, as well as English. No matter the language, the message of Jesus' love will always be the same.

SHARING FAITH
with My Family

Sharing What I Learned

Look at the pictures below. Use each picture to tell your family what you learned in this chapter.

A Holy Spirit Window

With your family, design and color a stained-glass window that will remind everyone of the Holy Spirit.

The Story of the Church

Cut out this picture of Saint Paul. Glue it to a piece of cardboard or stiff paper. Fold and stand. Talk with your family about the life of Saint Paul. Keep this picture in a special place.

Fold

Fold

Visit Sadlier's

www.WeBelieveweb.com

Connect to the Catechism
For adult background and reflection, see paragraphs 729, 731, 732, and 849.

5

WE GATHER

✝ **Leader:** Let us gather in a prayer circle. Sit in a comfortable position.

Become still . . . still . . . still.

Close your eyes. Now, as you breathe out, whisper the name

Jesus

Jesus

Jesus.

Have you ever wanted to be a leader of a group or team? What does a leader do?

WE BELIEVE
The apostles led the Church.

The apostles lived with Jesus for three years. They knew how kind and caring he was. They ate and drank with him. They heard his words every day. They saw him heal the sick and raise the dead.

Wherever they went, the apostles began to tell everyone about Jesus Christ. They baptized all those who believed in Jesus. In each place that they visited, the apostles gathered these new Christians together. This is how they formed the Church. The apostles had to move on to continue the work of Jesus so they chose leaders in each place.

There is a wonderful book in the New Testament that tells the story of the work of the apostles in the early Church. It is called the Acts of the Apostles. In that book, we read that the early Christians listened to the teachings of the apostles and looked after one another "according to each one's need." (Acts of the Apostles 2:45) The Church grew because Christians loved and served one another.

 Name one way the apostles were good leaders of the Church.

_____

_____

PHILIPPI

CORINTH

EPHESUS

Key Words

Acts of the Apostles
(p. 250)

gospel (p. 251)

The disciples of Jesus share the good news.

The followers of Jesus wanted everyone they met to know the good news of Jesus Christ:

• Jesus is the Son of God. He came into the world to become one of us and show us, in person, the love of God.

• Jesus is the Savior of the whole world. All of us have been saved by the life, death, and Resurrection of Jesus Christ.

Those who believed and accepted the good news were baptized and became members of the Church. They listened to what the apostles told them about Jesus and his teachings. They gathered together to share the Eucharist and "devoted themselves to the teaching of the apostles." (Acts of the Apostles 2:42)

Another word for "good news" is *gospel*. The gospel is the good news that we are saved by Jesus Christ, the Son of God. Like the first disciples, we are called to share the gospel.

Work with a partner. On a strip of paper, write some good news about Jesus that you wish to share with someone. Gather in a circle and share your good news. Then make a gospel chain.

The followers of Jesus stood up for their faith.

The Church began at a time when many countries were part of the Roman Empire. The Romans wanted everyone to worship their false gods. But the Christians would worship only the one, true God. Many Romans thought the Christians were a threat to the emperor's power. Soon the Christians were forced to worship Roman gods or face death.

The Roman leaders tried to make the Christians give up their faith in Jesus Christ. Many Christians were put in prison because they would not. Some Christians even died for their faith. We call people who die for their faith **martyrs**.

Name someone you know who stands up for his or her faith. Pray for that person.

Many of our ancestors in faith are examples of holiness.

Millions of Christians have lived before us. They are our ancestors in faith. Because of their holy lives the Church calls some of them saints.

Saints Perpetua and Felicity are two examples of holiness. Both of them were preparing to become Christians in the early years of the Church. Because of this they were arrested and treated terribly by the guards. Yet they both refused to worship Roman gods. They continued to believe in Jesus even when they were put to death.

Key Word

martyrs (p. 252)

54

Saint Augustine lived in North Africa. He was very popular when he was young. He was so busy enjoying himself that he never had time to think about God. As he grew older, he began to feel that his life had no meaning.

Augustine realized that God could give his life meaning. Augustine began to change. His love and need for God continued to grow. Augustine became a bishop and one of the Church's great writers.

These saints may have lived years ago, but their call to be holy is the same as ours is today.

Benozzo Gozzoli (1420–1497), *Saint Augustine*

WE RESPOND

How can you follow the saints who are our models of holiness? Circle the words in the letter box that will complete the sentences. Write the words on the lines provided.

F A I R J U S T
H E L P E X O H
A W O R S H I P
I T S A U M N D
R G O Y S R U O

We can tell others about _____.

We can _____ and _____ together, especially at Mass.

We can try to _____ others, especially those most in need.

We can be _____ and _____ to all people.

Review

Circle the letter beside the correct answer.

1. The word *gospel* means _____.

   a. Church   **b.** apostle   **c.** good news

2. In the Acts of the Apostles we read about the work of _____.

   a. Saint Felicity   **b.** the early Church   **c.** Saint Augustine

3. A _____ is someone who dies for the faith.

   a. martyr   **b.** disciple   **c.** follower

4. Augustine and Perpetua are examples of _____.

   a. apostles   **b.** martyrs   **c.** holiness

Use your own words to complete this sentence.

5. The early Christians gathered together to _____

   _____

   _____

   _____

ASSESSMENT

Some of your ancestors in faith were saints and martyrs. Use the Internet or library to find out what you can about a saint or a martyr. Draw a picture of a way that saint lived a holy life. Or write a paragraph telling about the ways that person was a faithful follower of Jesus.

We Respond in Faith

Reflect & Pray

I want to share the good news of Jesus Christ. This week, I especially want to share the part of the good news that tells us that

_____

I will need help to do this. I will ask one of my ancestors in faith (a saint I have learned about from my parents or in school) to help me.

Dear _____

_____

Key Words

Acts of the Apostles (p. 250)
gospel (p. 251)
martyrs (p. 252)

Remember

- The apostles led the Church.
- The disciples of Jesus share the good news.
- The followers of Jesus stood up for their faith.
- Many of our ancestors in faith are examples of holiness.

OUR CATHOLIC LIFE

All Saints

By our Baptism we have all been called to become holy, or to become saints. We must decide on how we can be holy, how we can love, and how we can serve God. We can look at the lives of the saints, the holy women and men who have gone before us. The saints come from every country, race, and culture. Their lives were filled with love for God. On November 1, All Saints' Day, the Church remembers all of the saints who are already celebrating God's life and love in heaven.

SHARING FAITH
with My Family

Sharing What I Learned

Look at the pictures below. Use each picture to tell your family what you learned in this chapter.

Family Prayer
(Lead your family in this prayer.)

Let us pray.
Jesus, we thank you for bringing us good news. My good news today is _____.
(Each family member adds his or her good news.)

Jesus, help us to spread your good news. You are the Lord and Savior of the world.

Amen.

Fold

Fold

The Story of the Church

Cut out this blank figure outline. Make one for each family member. Have everyone draw their likeness in the outlines. Fold and stand. How can your family follow Jesus?

Visit Sadlier's
www.WeBelieveweb.com

 Connect to the Catechism
For adult background and reflection, see paragraphs 551, 763, 769, and 2030.

The Church Year

HOSANNA

"Hosanna!
Blessed is he who comes in
the name of the Lord!"

Mark 11:9

The Church year celebrates Jesus.

WE GATHER

What holidays do you and your family celebrate during the year? What holy days do you celebrate? Name some of your favorite days of celebration.

WE BELIEVE

All during the year, we gather to praise and thank God for his many gifts. We remember and celebrate the amazing things Jesus did for us. The seasons of the Church year help us to grow as followers of Jesus. The seasons help us to grow in faith.

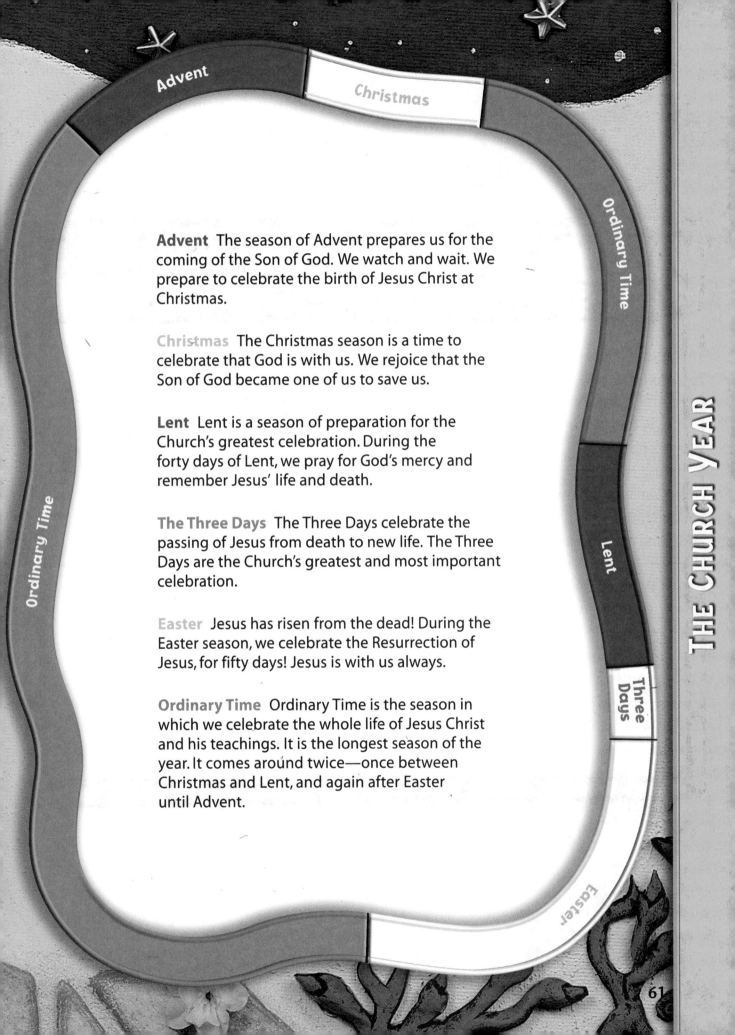

Advent The season of Advent prepares us for the coming of the Son of God. We watch and wait. We prepare to celebrate the birth of Jesus Christ at Christmas.

Christmas The Christmas season is a time to celebrate that God is with us. We rejoice that the Son of God became one of us to save us.

Lent Lent is a season of preparation for the Church's greatest celebration. During the forty days of Lent, we pray for God's mercy and remember Jesus' life and death.

The Three Days The Three Days celebrate the passing of Jesus from death to new life. The Three Days are the Church's greatest and most important celebration.

Easter Jesus has risen from the dead! During the Easter season, we celebrate the Resurrection of Jesus, for fifty days! Jesus is with us always.

Ordinary Time Ordinary Time is the season in which we celebrate the whole life of Jesus Christ and his teachings. It is the longest season of the year. It comes around twice—once between Christmas and Lent, and again after Easter until Advent.

Advent

Christmas

Ordinary Time

Lent

Three Days

Ordinary Time

Easter

Look at the Church year time line on page 61. Then write the answers to these questions.

What is the shortest season of the year?	Three days
What is the longest season of the year?	Ordinary time
In what season do we celebrate that Jesus rose from the dead and is with us always?	Easter
What season of the year comes around twice?	Ordinary time
What season of the year are we in now?	Ordinary time
What season will we celebrate next?	Advent

What is one great way to celebrate that Jesus is always with us?

✝ We Respond in Prayer

Leader: Blessed be the name of the Lord.

All: Now and for ever.

Reader: A reading from the holy Gospel according to Matthew

Jesus said to his disciples, "Behold, I am with you always, until the end of the age." (Matthew 28:20)

The Gospel of the Lord.

All: Praise to you, Lord Jesus Christ.

Leader: Glory to the Father, and to the Son, and to the Holy Spirit.

All: Now and for ever. Amen.

🎵 Jesus Is with Us

Chorus
Jesus is with us today,
Beside us to guide us today.
Jesus teaches us,
Jesus heals us, for we are his Church;
we are his chosen; we are the children of God.

Jesus teaches us to love one another,
To care for our brothers and sisters in need.
For when we show kindness to others,
We are God's children indeed. (Chorus)

SHARING FAITH
with My Family

Sharing What I Learned

Look at the pictures below. Use them to tell your family what you learned in this chapter.

Around the Table

Share with your family the liturgical colors for each season. Plan a way to include the color of the season in your household decorating. You might want to make paper chains, napkin-holders, or place mats. On your decorations, write the name of the season you are celebrating.

A Family Blessing

Be our shelter, Lord, when we are at home, our companion when we are away, and our welcome guest when we return. And at last receive us into the dwelling place you have prepared for us in your Father's house, where you live for ever and ever. Amen.

Visit Sadlier's

www.WeBelieveweb.com

 Connect to the Catechism
For adult background and reflection, see paragraph 1168.

Ordinary Time

Advent Christmas Ordinary Time Lent Three Days Easter Ordinary Time

"Lord, it is good
to give thanks to you."

Responsorial Psalm, Eighth Sunday
in Ordinary Time

In Ordinary Time, we celebrate the life and teachings of Jesus Christ.

WE GATHER

Can you remember the names of all the seasons in the liturgical year?

Which season is the Church in right now?

WE BELIEVE

Ordinary Time is a special time in the Church. During this season, we celebrate everything about Jesus! We hear about his teaching, his love, and his forgiveness. We also learn to be his followers.

Ordinary Time is the longest season of the Church year. It lasts about thirty-three or thirty-four weeks. It is called Ordinary Time because the weeks are "ordered," or named in number order. For example, the First Sunday in Ordinary Time is followed by the Second Sunday in Ordinary Time, and so on.

On the Sundays of Ordinary Time, and on the weekdays, too, the priest wears green vestments. Green is a sign of new life and hope.

On Sundays and weekdays in Ordinary Time, we learn about Jesus and his teachings by listening to the Scripture readings. Sometimes we hear events in the life of Jesus. Sometimes we hear a story Jesus told.

Together make a list of some of the events in the life of Jesus and a list of some stories he told.

_____

_____

_____

_____

Then in groups talk about your favorite events or stories. Act out one for the rest of the class.

During Ordinary Time, we learn more about Jesus and his teachings so that we can become more like him. Jesus shares himself with us in the sacraments. As Jesus did, we pray, love others, and work for justice and peace.

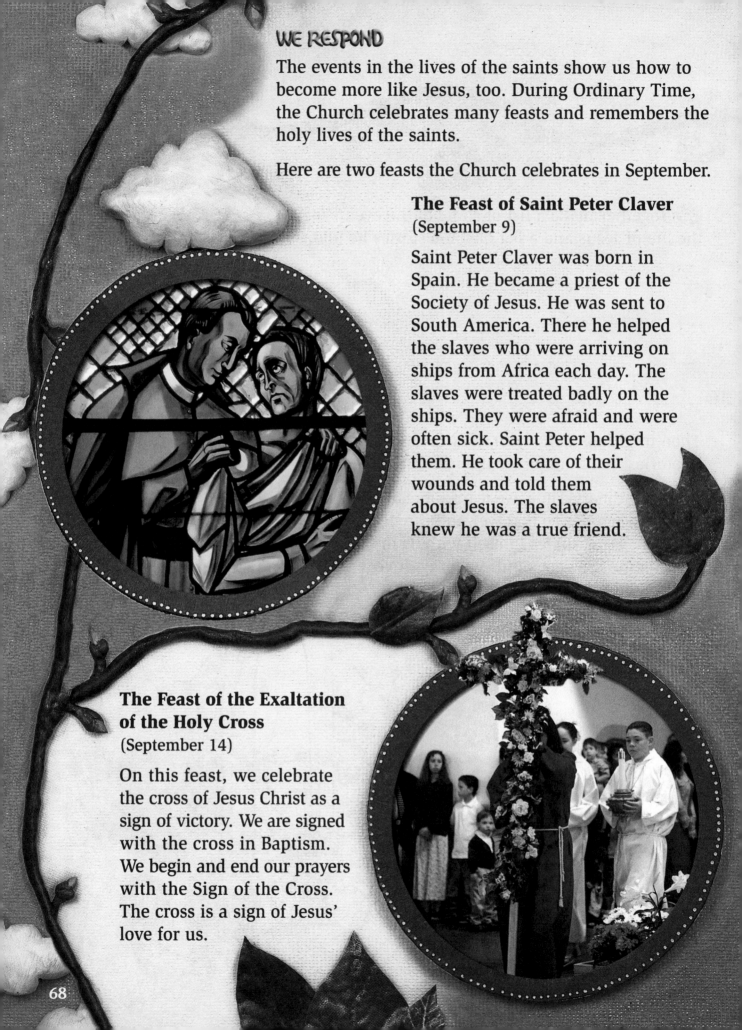

WE RESPOND

The events in the lives of the saints show us how to become more like Jesus, too. During Ordinary Time, the Church celebrates many feasts and remembers the holy lives of the saints.

Here are two feasts the Church celebrates in September.

The Feast of Saint Peter Claver
(September 9)

Saint Peter Claver was born in Spain. He became a priest of the Society of Jesus. He was sent to South America. There he helped the slaves who were arriving on ships from Africa each day. The slaves were treated badly on the ships. They were afraid and were often sick. Saint Peter helped them. He took care of their wounds and told them about Jesus. The slaves knew he was a true friend.

The Feast of the Exaltation of the Holy Cross
(September 14)

On this feast, we celebrate the cross of Jesus Christ as a sign of victory. We are signed with the cross in Baptism. We begin and end our prayers with the Sign of the Cross. The cross is a sign of Jesus' love for us.

✝ We Respond in Prayer

Leader: Let us pray now to honor the holy cross of Jesus. As we sing a song of joy and victory, let us process to our place of prayer.

🎵 **We Sing Your Glory**

We sing your glory,
   sing your praise.
We sing your glory,
   sing your praise.
We sing your glory,
   we sing your glory.
Glory, glory and praise!

Reader: "The grace of the Lord Jesus Christ and the love of God and the fellowship of the holy Spirit be with all of you."
(2 Corinthians 13:13)

All: And also with you.

Reader: Jesus, your cross is a sign of your love for us and for the whole world.

All: Jesus, make us signs of your love.

Leader: Father, we rejoice in the gifts of love we have received through the holy cross of Jesus your Son. Open our hearts to share his life and continue to bless us with his love. We ask this in the name of Jesus the Lord.

All: Amen.

SHARING FAITH
with My Family

Sharing What I Learned

Look at the pictures below. Use each picture to tell your family what you have learned in this chapter.

Around the Table

How will your family work together to follow Jesus in Ordinary Time? Post your ideas on the refrigerator.

Here are some ideas:

• Pray for world peace.

• Share a special meal and invite someone you know who may be lonely.

• Plan a trip to a beautiful shrine.

Family Prayer for Ordinary Time

Jesus taught us to pray to his Father. We pray in the Our Father, "thy kingdom come." Pray the Our Father together. As you pray it, ask Jesus to help you show others that his Kingdom has begun.

Visit Sadlier's
www.WeBelieveweb.com

Connect to the Catechism
For adult background and reflection, see paragraph 1163.

Assessment

Fill in the circle beside the correct answer.

1. Jesus is both divine and _____.

    ○ unkind   ○ human   ○ sinful

2. _____ allows us to believe what we cannot see or feel or touch.

    ○ Faith   ○ Sin   ○ Scripture

3. When Jesus comes again, he will judge _____.

    ○ just sinners   ○ all people   ○ only his followers

4. Jesus' raising Lazarus from the dead was a _____.

    ○ mission   ○ miracle   ○ promise

5. The saints are our _____ in faith.

    ○ followers   ○ ancestors   ○ martyrs

6. _____ made many trips to build up Christian communities throughout the world.

    ○ Mary   ○ Stephen   ○ Paul

Use your own words to answer these questions.

7–8. What are some ways we love and care for others as Jesus did?

_____

_____

9–10. What is the Acts of the Apostles?

_____

_____

Complete the crossword puzzle.

Across

1. Special job

2. "One who is sent"

3. "Good news" that we are saved by Jesus

Down

1. People who die for their faith

4. Life with God forever

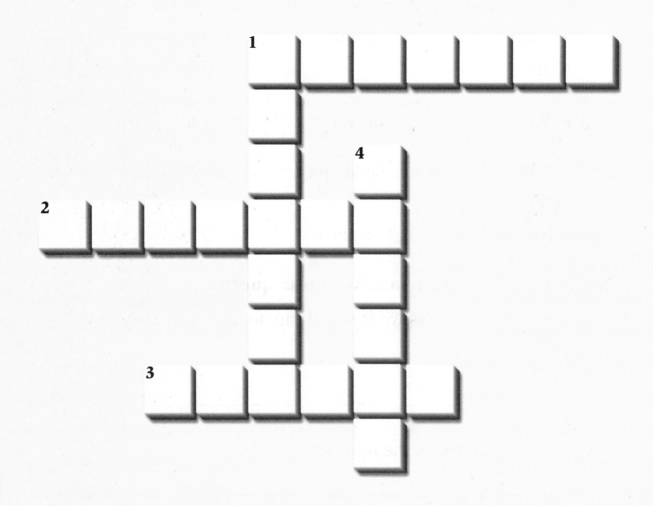

We Are Members of the Church

Turn Down the Sound

An important aspect of teaching children to pray is helping them to be quiet. This means turning down the sound internally as well as externally.

External quiet. We live in a noisy world. Television, cell phones, computers, background music, and traffic are just some of the sources of sound that engulf us. It becomes such a part of our routine that we often become immune to it. Help your child embrace the joy of silence by introducing a daily "quiet time" in your home. Turn off all electronic media for a set period of time. Encourage everyone to take part in a quiet activity, such as reading or working a puzzle. You are likely to find the family looking forward to and wanting to extend this "quiet time."

Internal quiet. As these external times of quiet are achieved, help your child develop ways of being still. Before turning out the lights at bedtime, spend time together, eyes closed, thinking over the best part of the day. During the day, go outside with your child, perhaps to a park or garden. Sit in silence together, and savor the feeling of interior peace.

Cultivated as a habit, the ability to be quiet is one that will give rise to deeper and richer prayer—both for your child and for you. Are you ready for it?

What Your Child Will Learn in Unit 2

In Unit 2, the children will come to more of an understanding that they are members of the Church. The four marks of the Church (one, holy, catholic, and apostolic) are explained, as are the images of the Church as the people of God and as the Body of Christ. The children will learn the Apostles' Creed as well as ways that the Church guides us—especially through Catholic social teaching. Prayer is another focal point in Unit 2. The children will understand the types of prayer, and the difference between liturgical and private prayer. They will see how the Church continues the prayer of Jesus throughout the world. There is an entire chapter devoted to the parish. The children will discover the parish as a family in Christ and appreciate the various ministries as well as the purposes of a parish. Lastly, Unit 2 talks about the meaning and types of vocations found in the Church. The emphasis here is on the fact that, whether one is single, married, in the priesthood, or a religious brother or sister, God calls each one of us to lead a life of holiness.

Plan & Preview

▶ This unit's *Family Pages* offer prayer cards that can be taped to the refrigerator door for all to see and pray. You will need scissors to cut out the prayer, one per chapter, and transparent tape.

A Prayer to the Holy Spirit

Come, Holy Spirit, be with our family.
Bring each one of us closer to Jesus each day.
Help us to listen to your voice.
Come, Holy Spirit, be with us in everything we do.
Amen.

The Universal Prayer

Lord, I believe in you: increase my faith.
I trust in you: strengthen my trust.
I love you: let me love you more and more.
I am sorry for my sins: deepen my sorrow.

Guide me by your wisdom,
Correct me with your justice,
Comfort me with your mercy,
Protect me with your power.

I want to do what you ask of me:
In the way you ask,
For as long as you ask,
Because you ask it.

Amen.

(attributed to Pope Clement XI, edited version)

From the Catechism

"Authority, stability, and a life of relationships within the family constitute the foundations for freedom, security, and fraternity within society."

(*Catechism of the Catholic Church*, 2207)

Bible Q & A

Q: My child will be learning about Jesus at prayer. What can I read to him to help him understand the meaning of prayer?

—Scottsville, Kentucky

A: Prayer is a vital part of Jesus' message. To learn more, read Matthew 6:5–8 and 7:7–11 as well as Philippians 4:4–7.

Note the Quote

"Prayer in my opinion is nothing else than an intimate sharing between friends; it means taking time frequently to be alone with Him who we know loves us."

Saint Teresa of Avila

The Church Has Four Marks

WE GATHER

✝ **Leader:** Jesus spoke to the crowds that followed him. He speaks to each of us, too. Let us listen to his words.

Reader: "I am the light of the world." (John 8:12)

Will you follow me?

All: Yes, Jesus, we will follow you.

Reader: "I am the bread of life." (John 6:35)

Will you receive me?

All: Yes, Jesus, we will receive you.

Reader: "I am the resurrection and the life." (John 11:25)

Do you believe in me?

All: Yes, Jesus, we believe in you. Amen.

☀ Think about the school teams or clubs that you can join. Who are the leaders of these groups? What do they do?

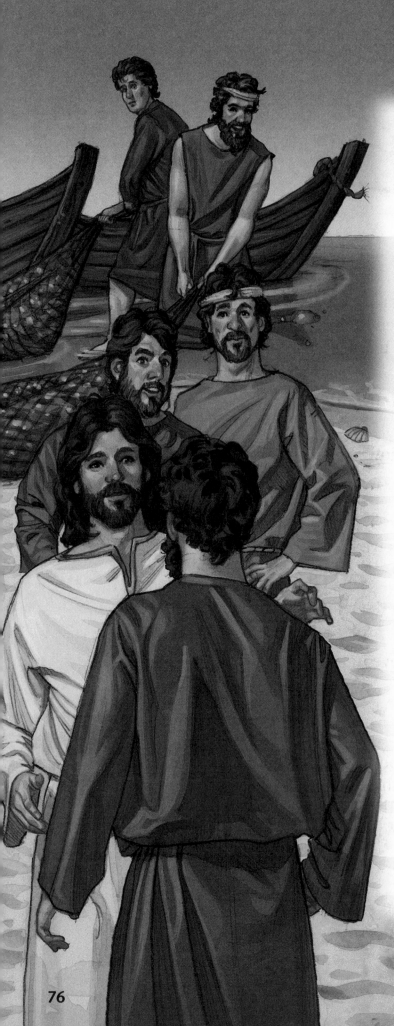

WE BELIEVE

Jesus chose the apostles to lead the Church.

One of Jesus' apostles was named Simon. Jesus changed Simon's name to Peter, which means "rock." Jesus chose Peter to be the leader of the apostles. He told Peter, "You are Peter, and upon this rock I will build my church." (Matthew 16:18)

The apostles are Peter, Andrew, James and John (sons of Zebedee), Philip, Bartholomew, Thomas, Matthew, James (the son of Alphaeus), Thaddeus, Simon, and Judas Iscariot. Later Matthias took the place of Judas.

After Jesus' Ascension the apostles told the people all that Jesus had said and done. They traveled from place to place teaching what Jesus had taught them.

In every location the apostles gathered the baptized into communities. The Church grew, and the first members of the Church looked to Peter and the apostles as their leaders.

Look at the picture on page 77. In the space, write something you think the apostle told people about Jesus.

What will you tell people you know about Jesus?

The pope and bishops are the successors of the apostles.

Like Jesus, the apostles chose leaders to succeed them. A *successor* is one who succeeds, or takes the place of, another. These new leaders would take the place of the apostles and continue their work.

The apostles gave these leaders the same authority that Jesus had given to them. Strengthened by the Holy Spirit, these leaders became the successors of the apostles.

As time passed each of these leaders was given the title of bishop. **Bishops** are the successors of the apostles. The bishops continue to lead the Church. They lead local areas of the Church called **dioceses**.

The **pope** is the bishop of the diocese of Rome in Italy. He continues the leadership of Peter. Together with all the bishops, he leads and guides the whole Catholic Church.

 Talk about what you know about your bishop, your diocese, and the pope.

Find out more about the pope and Vatican City. Check the Vatican Web site at www.vatican.net.

Key Words
bishops (p. 250)
dioceses (p. 250)
pope (p. 253)

bishops (p. 250)
dioceses (p. 250)
pope (p. 253)

As Catholics...

The pope lives in Vatican City, in Rome, Italy. He is the leader of the whole Catholic Church. So in a way the whole world is his parish. He goes to places around the world to teach the good news of Jesus Christ and to seek peace. He encourages people to treat one another with respect. He also asks for help for those who are in need.

The Church is one and holy.

The Church is one, holy, catholic, and apostolic. We call these characteristics the **marks of the Church**.

The Church is *one*, a community called together by God. Through the Church, God strengthens us to live and worship together.

All members of the Church are united by Baptism. We gather to celebrate the sacraments. We share with one another and serve together.

The Church is *holy*. God is all good and holy. God shares his holiness with the Church. Through Baptism all members of the Church receive a share in God's life. This share in God's life makes us holy.

As members of the Church we grow in holiness when we celebrate the sacraments. We also grow in holiness when we love God and others as Jesus did.

What is one way the Church is a community?

Key Word

marks of the Church (p. 252)

The Church is catholic and apostolic.

The Church is catholic. The word *catholic* means "universal." The Church is open to all people. It is universal.

Jesus sent his apostles out to every part of the world. They spread the gospel to everyone, and the Church continued to grow. Even today people everywhere are invited and welcomed to become members of the Church. There are Catholics on every continent and in every country.

The Church is *apostolic*. The word *apostolic* comes from the word *apostle*. Jesus chose the apostles to be the first leaders of the Church. Their mission was to teach the good news and to baptize believers. By Baptism all members of the Church share in the work of spreading the good news of Christ.

The bishops continue the mission of the apostles in three very important ways.

- They *teach*. The bishops are the official teachers of the Church. They make sure that the members of the Church know and believe the teachings of Jesus.

- They *lead*. The bishops are the main leaders of the Church.

- They *sanctify*. The bishops work to make the people of God holy. They do this through prayer, preaching, and the celebration of the sacraments.

WE RESPOND

Draw a picture to show one of the four marks of the Church.

Match the words or phrases in Column A to the correct descriptions in Column B.

A   **B**

1. marks of the Church   _____ successors of the apostles

                                       _____ twelve disciples chosen by
                                                Jesus to share in his mission

2. pope

                                       _____ four characteristics that
                                                describe the Church
3. bishops

4. apostles   _____ continues the leadership
                                         of Peter

Complete this sentence.

5. The Church is one community _____

_____

_____

_____

Explain in your own words the marks of the Church. Make a design or logo showing that the Church is one, holy, catholic, and apostolic.

We Respond in Faith ✝

Reflect & Pray

Describe how the Church grew during the time of the apostles.

_____

_____

Jesus, I believe in you and love you. Help me to live as a loving member of the Church. Help me especially to

_____

_____

Key Words

bishops (p. 250)
dioceses (p. 251)
pope (p. 253)
marks of the Church (p. 252)

Remember

- Jesus chose the apostles to lead the Church.
- The pope and bishops are the successors of the apostles.
- The Church is one and holy.
- The Church is catholic and apostolic.

OUR CATHOLIC LIFE

Blessed Pope John XXIII

Angelo Roncalli became Pope John XXIII at 76 years of age. No one thought he would do much. But he surprised everyone with his energy and great spirit. He called the bishops from all over the world to gather together in Rome. This meeting was known as the *Second Vatican Council*. The pope and bishops worked together to strengthen the one, holy, catholic, and apostolic Church. They called the Church to reach out to other religions and especially to the poor. The council called us to be God's people.

SHARING FAITH
with My Family

Sharing What I Learned

Look at the pictures below. Use each picture to tell your family what you learned in this chapter.

A Prayer for the Church

Father,

we pray for the Church,

and for us, its members.

Make us one.

Make us holy.

Make us catholic.

Make us apostolic.

We ask this in the name of

your Son, Jesus Christ. Amen.

Marks of Our Family

The Church has four marks, or characteristics. Talk with your family about what makes your family special. Write your family characteristics in the spaces below.

The _____ **Family**

_____   _____

_____   _____

Refrigerator Prayer Card

(Pray this prayer with your family.)

Cut out this card. Place it where everyone can see it. Each time you see this card, pray the prayer again.

Visit Sadlier's

www.WeBelieveweb.com

Connect to the Catechism
For adult background and reflection, see paragraphs 765, 880, 811, 823, 830, and 857.

WE GATHER

✝ **Leader:** God, we are your people.

All: We are your Church.

Leader: Keep us faithful to you.

All: We are your faithful followers.

Leader: Help us to do your work on earth.

All: We want to share your good news with others.

🎵 **They'll Know We Are Christians**

We will walk with each other,
We will walk hand in hand,
We will walk with each other,
We will walk hand in hand,
And together we'll spread the news
that God is in our land.
And they'll know we are Christians
by our love, by our love,
Yes, they'll know we are Christians
by our love.

☀ Name some good things about being a member of your family or your class.

WE BELIEVE

The Church is the Body of Christ and the people of God.

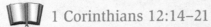 1 Corinthians 12:14–21

Saint Paul explained to the people that the Church is the *Body of Christ* on earth. All the parts in a person's body work together. The ear does not say, "Because I am not an eye I do not belong to the body." The eye does not say to the hand, "I do not need you." (1 Corinthians 12:16, 21) Each part of the body needs all the other parts.

Like a human body, the Church has many parts, or members. One part cannot say to another, "I do not need you!" or "You are not like me, so you do not belong." Everyone in the Church is an important part of the Body of Christ. We are united through our love for and belief in Jesus Christ.

God has chosen us to be his children, brothers and sisters of Jesus. Through our Baptism, we are brought into the Church. In the New Testament the Church is described as "God's people." (1 Peter 2:10) As the *people of God*, we try our best to love God and love one another. We try to share the good news of Jesus with everyone in the world.

Look at the pictures. How are these people showing that they are the people of God?

_____

_____

_____

_____

We profess our faith through the Apostles' Creed.

Apostles' Creed

I believe in God, the Father almighty,
    creator of heaven and earth.

I believe in Jesus Christ, his only
        Son, our Lord.
    He was conceived by the power
        of the Holy Spirit
        and born of the Virgin Mary.
    He suffered under Pontius Pilate,
        was crucified, died, and was buried.
    He descended to the dead.
    On the third day he rose again.
    He ascended into heaven,
        and is seated at the right hand
        of the Father.
    He will come again to judge
        the living and the dead.

I believe in the Holy Spirit,
    the holy catholic Church,
    the communion of saints,
    the forgiveness of sins,
    the resurrection of the body,
    and the life everlasting.
Amen.

We state our belief in the Blessed Trinity: God the Father, God the Son, and God the Holy Spirit.

We state our belief that God the Son, the second Person of the Blessed Trinity, became one of us and died to save us.

We state our belief in the holy catholic Church that Jesus gave us. When we pray the Apostles' Creed we say together as the Church that we are one in faith and love.

As the Church grew, the beliefs about Jesus and his teachings were written down in statements called *creeds*. One of the first creeds is called the **Apostles' Creed**. It is based on the teachings of Jesus Christ and the faith of the apostles.

Each time we pray the Apostles' Creed, we profess our faith. To *profess* means "to state what we believe."

Apostles' Creed
(p. 250)

With a partner talk about the ways we show our Catholic beliefs.

The Holy Spirit guides the Church.

Jesus knew it would be difficult for the apostles to remember everything he had taught them. So he promised the apostles that "the holy Spirit that the Father will send in my name–he will teach you everything and remind you of all that [I] told you." (John 14:26) With the help of the Holy Spirit, the apostles were able to speak the truth about Jesus.

Today the Holy Spirit continues to guide the Church. The Holy Spirit guides the pope and bishops to teach the truth about Jesus. They do this by their words, writings, and actions. The pope and the bishops are the official teachers for the whole Church.

At certain times the pope gathers together all the bishops throughout the world. They make important decisions about the Church's faith and life.

Often the pope writes letters to the Church and to the whole world. These letters are about Catholic beliefs and how to live as Catholics in the world today.

Name something you have learned about Jesus and the Church. Who taught you?

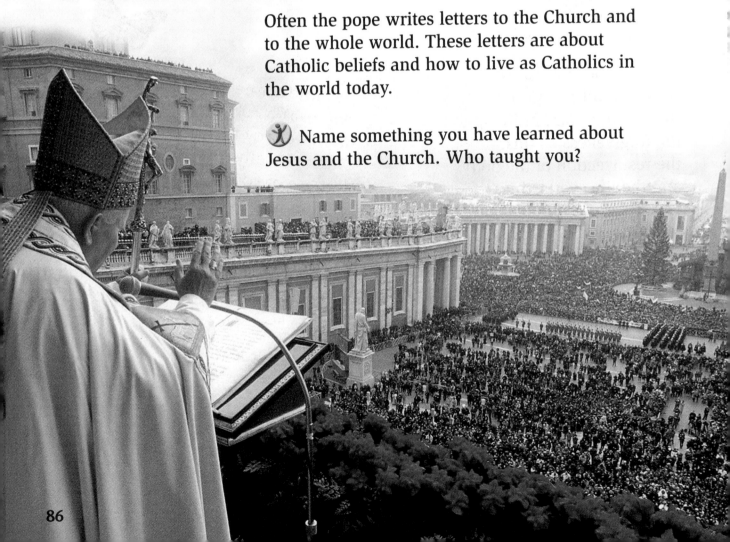

The Church continues to teach the true message of Jesus.

The Church teaches what Jesus taught:

- God loves and cares for everyone.

- We are to love God with our whole heart.

- We are to love our neighbors as ourselves.

Some of the Church's teaching is known as *Catholic social teaching.* This teaching tells us that we are all made in God's image and have certain human rights. For example, we all have the right to life, food, housing, and safety. We have the right to be educated and to be treated equally.

These human rights are an important part of justice. **Justice** is treating everyone fairly and with respect. The justice that Jesus taught reminds us that we are all part of the human family. What helps or hurts one part of the family affects everyone.

We all have certain responsibilities to one another. For example, we have a responsibility to live together in peace. We have a responsibility to share the good things of the world. We have a responsibility to respect and care for one another.

WE RESPOND

What can you do this week to treat everyone fairly at home?

_____

in school?

_____

in your parish?

_____

Key Word

justice (p. 251)

87

Review

Grade 3
Chapter 9

Write T if the sentence is true. Write F if the sentence is false.

1. The Church is the Body of Christ on earth. _____

2. Justice is a statement of beliefs. _____

3. The Holy Spirit helps the pope and bishops teach the truth about Jesus and our Catholic faith. _____

4. We have a responsibility to care only about the Catholics in our diocese. _____

Complete this sentence.

5. Catholic social teaching tells us _____

_____

_____

_____

_____

_____

Make a poster to show that the Church is the Body of Christ. Explain why every person is important.

We Respond in Faith

Reflect & Pray

What are some ways that you can act with justice in school? at home?

Jesus sent the Holy Spirit to guide us and to help us to remember his teachings.

Holy Spirit, be with me and guide me, especially when

_____

_____

Key Words

Apostles' Creed (p. 250)
justice (p. 251)

Remember

- The Church is the Body of Christ and the people of God.
- We profess our faith through the Apostles' Creed.
- The Holy Spirit guides the Church.
- The Church continues to teach the true message of Jesus.

OUR CATHOLIC LIFE

Catholic Charities USA

Justice is why Catholic Charities USA helps over ten million needy people throughout the United States each year. At food pantries, members of this group offer free bags of groceries for those in need. They offer counseling, daycare programs, and job training. They also work for justice for all people. Catholics can participate in the work of Catholic Charities USA by volunteering their time and by donating food, clothing, and money.

SHARING FAITH
with My Family

Sharing What I Learned

Look at the pictures below. Use each picture to tell your family what you learned in this chapter.

A Prayer to the Holy Spirit

Come, Holy Spirit,
be with our family.
Bring each one of us
closer to Jesus each day.
Help us to listen
to your voice.

Come, Holy Spirit,
be with us
in everything we do.
Amen.

Make Justice Part of Your Life

Share the Church's teachings on justice with your family. Brainstorm ways your family can show respect for one another.

How can your family share good things with those who have less? Brainstorm ways that your family can be peacemakers in your neighborhood.

Refrigerator Prayer Card

(Pray this prayer with your family.)

Cut out this card. Place it where everyone can see it. Each time you see this card, pray the prayer again.

Visit Sadlier's

www.WeBelieveweb.com

Connect to the Catechism
For adult background and reflection, see paragraphs 782, 194, 798, and 771.

The Church Prays

10

WE GATHER

✝ **Leader:** Be still and quiet. Place your hands on your knees with your palms up.

Talk to God in your heart. Tell him anything you wish. Ask God for what you need, and ask his blessing on those you love.

All: (Pray quietly.)

Leader: Lift up your hands as a sign of your prayer rising to God.

All: Let my prayer be incense before you.

(Psalm 141:2a)

When someone you love is far away, how can you stay in touch?

WE BELIEVE
Jesus teaches his followers how to pray.

Jesus is the son of God. Jesus is divine because he is God. He is also Mary's son. Jesus is human like us in every way except he is without sin.

Jesus had to learn how to walk, talk, read, and write. Mary and Joseph also taught Jesus how to talk to God in prayer. **Prayer** is listening and talking to God.

Jesus prayed in the **synagogue**, the gathering place where Jewish people pray and learn about God. Jesus also worshiped in the Temple in Jerusalem. Other times he went off by himself to pray. Sometimes he prayed with his family or his disciples.

The disciples wanted to learn how to pray as Jesus did. One day they said to him, "Lord, teach us to pray." (Luke 11:1) So Jesus taught them this prayer:

> Our Father, who art in heaven,
> hallowed be thy name;
> thy kingdom come;
> thy will be done on earth
>   as it is in heaven.
> Give us this day our daily bread;
> and forgive us our trespasses
> as we forgive those who trespass
>   against us;
> and lead us not into temptation,
> but deliver us from evil. Amen.

This prayer is the Lord's Prayer. We also call it the Our Father. It is the greatest example of prayer for the Church.

Use your own words to tell what we pray for when we pray the Lord's Prayer.

We can pray with others or by ourselves.

We often come together to worship God. We gather with others to celebrate the liturgy, the official public prayer of the Church. Each celebration, such as the Mass and the sacraments, is an action of the whole Church. Together as the Church, we worship the Blessed Trinity. We pray with Christ and with the whole Church, the Body of Christ.

Sometimes we pray alone just as Jesus did. We call this personal prayer. We can pray at any time and in any place. We can pray prayers such as the Our Father and the Hail Mary. We can also pray with our own words. God listens to us when we pray. He knows what we need.

Draw one way your family likes to pray.

Key Word

prayer (p. 253)

synagogue (p. 253)

liturgy (p. 251)

There are different kinds of prayer.

Think of a time when something was so beautiful or amazing that it made you think "Wow!" That feeling can become a *prayer of praise*. "O God, you are wonderful!"

Think of a time when you passed a difficult test or when you felt better after being sick. You felt grateful that God had been so good to you. You said, "Thank you so much, O Lord!" This is a *prayer of thanksgiving*.

There are other times when we know that we have done wrong, when we have sinned. We ask God for forgiveness. This is a *prayer of petition*.

A prayer is often prayed before a meal. We pray to God to bless the gift of our food. This is a *prayer of blessing*.

We can ask God to help our families, friends, and all the people in the world. This is a *prayer of intercession*.

Look at the pictures on these pages. Below each write the type of prayer that might be said: praise, thanksgiving, petition, blessing, or intercession.

_____

_____

The Church prays at all times.

Did you know that the Church is always at prayer? In one part of the world, children are beginning their school day by praying. Yet at the same time in another part of the world, children are saying their prayers before going to bed.

There are special prayers called the Liturgy of the Hours. These prayers are prayed seven different times during the day. So somewhere in the world, people are always praying the Liturgy of the Hours.

If we could travel around the world, we would be able to pray in different languages and in different ways. For example, in some countries, people pray by taking part in dances.

Other people would be praying by walking through the streets in processions. In some countries, we would see people praying at shrines set up along the roads. In other places, we would see people making journeys to holy places. These prayer-journeys are called **pilgrimages**.

The greatest prayer of the Church is the Mass. The Mass is the celebration of the Eucharist, the sacrament of the Body and Blood of Christ. It unites us all and leads us to live as Jesus' disciples.

WE RESPOND

In groups talk about some of the ways your parish prays. How do these ways help people to grow closer to God? Act out one of these ways for the rest of the class.

As Catholics...

We can pray with our bodies. We show respect for Jesus present in the Eucharist by genuflecting or bowing before the tabernacle. During Mass we pray by standing, kneeling, and sitting. At other times we pray with hands folded or with arms open wide. Sometimes people even pray by dancing!

How do you pray?

Key Word

pilgrimages (p. 252)

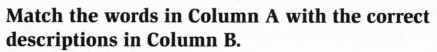

Review

Match the words in Column A with the correct descriptions in Column B.

A   **B**

1. pilgrimage   _____ gathering place where
                                         Jewish people pray and
                                         learn about God

2. prayer
                              _____ the official public prayer of
                                         the Church

3. synagogue   _____ a prayer-journey to a holy
                                         place

4. liturgy   _____ listening and talking to God

Answer the question.

5. How and when did Jesus pray?

_____

_____

_____

_____

ASSESSMENT

Imagine you are reading a book titled, "The Church Prays at All Times." Make up a list of the chapter titles for this book. Now design the page for the table of contents.

We Respond in Faith

Reflect & Pray

Jesus wants us to pray always. He is with us whenever we pray in his name. Finish the prayer.

Jesus, you are closer to me than I know. Be with me at all times. Especially help me to

_____

_____

_____

Key Words

prayer (p. 253)
synagogue (p. 253)
liturgy (p. 251)
pilgrimages (p. 252)

Remember

- Jesus teaches his followers how to pray.
- We can pray with others or by ourselves.
- There are different kinds of prayer.
- The Church prays at all times.

OUR CATHOLIC LIFE

General Intercessions

At every Mass, we pray the *general intercessions*. This is also called the *prayer of the faithful*. We remember the needs of the Church and all people in the world. We usually pray for: Church leaders and the whole Church; world leaders and world situations; our neighborhoods; the sick; and those who have died. Each person can also offer his or her own personal prayers.

SHARING FAITH
with My Family

Sharing What I Learned

Look at the pictures below. Use each picture to tell your family what you learned in this chapter.

Prayer of Praise
Praise and glory to the Father, the Son, and the Holy Spirit!

Prayer of Petition
We are sorry, Jesus. Help us to do better.

Prayer of Thanksgiving
Let us thank the Lord with all our hearts! Let us sing his praise!

Prayer of Intercession
Help us, Lord Jesus. Help our family and our friends, especially

_____.

Prayer of Blessing
Lord, bless these gifts that you have given our family.

Family Feedback

Tell your family about the different kinds of prayer. Then after Mass on Sunday, have your family talk about the prayers of the Mass that are:

- Prayers of Praise
- Prayers of Petition
- Prayers of Thanksgiving
- Prayers of Intercession
- Prayers of Blessing.

Refrigerator Prayer Card

Pray these prayers with your family. Cut out this card. Place it where everyone can see it. Each time you see this card, pray one of these prayers.

Visit Sadlier's
www.WeBelieveweb.com

Connect to the Catechism
For adult background and reflection, see paragraphs 2759, 2655, 2626, 2691, and 2697.

The Parish Is Our Home

11

WE GATHER

✝ **Leader:** Let us listen to the words of Jesus.

Reader: "I have called you friends. As I have loved you, so you also should love one another." (John 15:15; 13:34)

All: Thank you, Jesus, for calling us to be your friends and followers in the Church.

Reader: "For where two or three are gathered together in my name, there am I in the midst of them." (Matthew 18:20)

All: Thank you, Jesus, for our parish where we can gather in your name.

Reader: "Whatever you did for one of these least brothers of mine, you did for me." (Matthew 25:40)

All: Thank you, Jesus, for inviting us to do your work on earth. Help us to see you in all those in need. Amen.

☀ When does your whole family get together? Why?

We are SAINT LUKE'S PARISH

ThankYou JESUS!

WE BELIEVE
We belong to a parish.

A parish is like a family. A **parish** is a community of believers who worship and work together. It is made up of Catholics who usually live in the same neighborhood. It is part of a diocese which is led by a bishop.

The members of a parish share the same faith in Jesus Christ. Parish members:

- come together to celebrate the Mass and other sacraments

- come together to pray, learn, and grow in faith

- work together to meet the needs of their parish

- welcome people who want to become members of the Church. These people learn from others about the Catholic faith. They prepare for the sacraments of Baptism, Confirmation, and Eucharist.

You belong to a parish. In your parish there are many ways to live and grow as a Catholic.

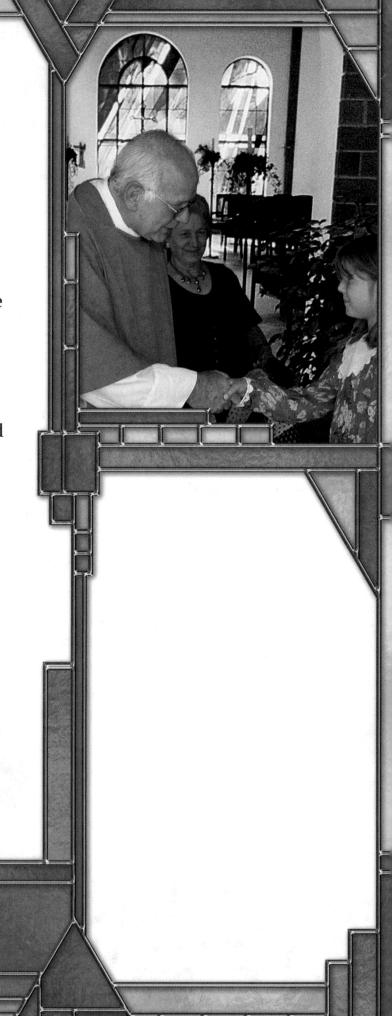 Draw or write about one time you took part in a parish activity.

Many people serve our parish.

Through our Baptism God calls each one of us. He calls us to do his work. This work is to bring the good news of Jesus Christ to others. Helping in our parish is a way to serve God and the Church.

A **pastor** is the priest who leads the parish in worship, prayer, and teaching. His most important work is to lead the parish in the celebration of the Mass. The parish might have other priests who work with the pastor. They also lead the parish in the celebration of the sacraments and in parish activities.

Sometimes the parish has a deacon. A **deacon** is a man who is not a priest but has received the sacrament of Holy Orders. He serves the parish by preaching, baptizing, and assisting the bishops and priests.

There are many ways of serving in your parish. These are called *ministries*. Some ministries are: catechist, director of youth services, director of social ministries, special minister of the Eucharist, director of music, altar server, and reader.

Can you name any other ministries? With a partner talk about how you and your family can help and serve your parish.

Key Words

parish (p. 252)
pastor (p. 252)
deacon (p. 250)

We are SAINT LUKE'S PARISH

Maria   Francis   Paul   Joanna

Go in Peace to Love and Serve the Lord!

Our parish worships together.

Celebrations are an important part of parish life. The Church has always gathered to celebrate the life, death, and Resurrection of Jesus. Participating in Mass is an important part of belonging to the Church.

Jesus said, "Where two or three are gathered together in my name, there am I in the midst of them." (Matthew 18:20) So when we gather as a parish, we are in the presence of Jesus. We gather to worship, to give thanks and praise to God.

Every time we celebrate Mass and the sacraments as a parish, we show our faith in Jesus. We show our love for him and for one another.

Name one thing you enjoy about worshiping with your parish.

Our parish cares for others.

Our parish worship encourages us to help others. At the end of each Mass, the priest or deacon says to us, "Go in peace to love and serve the Lord." We answer by saying, "Thanks be to God." But our real answer comes in our daily effort to help others.

We love and serve the Lord and others by:

- studying and learning more about our Catholic faith

- sharing the good news

- sharing what we have—our money, our time, and our talents—with one another

- caring for those in need—the sick, the poor, and the hungry

- making peace with others, even those who hurt us

- working for justice by treating all people fairly and with respect

- protecting the rights of people who cannot stand up for themselves.

All these actions are not just nice things to do. They are ways to show that we are true followers of Jesus Christ and members of his Body, the Church.

WE RESPOND

 What kinds of things take place in your parish? List some of these things using the letters below.

P
A
R _____
I _____
S _____
H _____

As Catholics...

Some parishes do not have priests to serve them. So the bishop of the diocese selects a *pastoral administrator* to serve the parish. This administrator leads parish activities. He or she guides the parish in religious education and prayer. However, the bishop always assigns a priest to celebrate Mass and the other sacraments at these parishes.

Do you know of any parishes with a pastoral administrator?

Write the word to complete the sentences.

1. A _____ is a community of believers who worship and work together.

2. The priest who leads a parish is called the _____.

3. Different ways of serving in a parish are called

    _____.

4. At the end of Mass, the priest or deacon sends us out to

    love and _____ the Lord.

Complete this sentence.

5. In our parish, we _____

    _____

    _____

    _____

    _____

    _____

Imagine a new family has joined your parish. Write at least three things you think they should know about your parish. How could you welcome them into your parish?

We Respond in Faith

Reflect & Pray

The parish is a community. What have I learned from my parish about being a member of the Church?

Finish this prayer.

Loving Father,
we belong to each other
just as we belong to you, our God.
Through our parish family, teach us to

_____

_____

Key Words

parish (p. 252)
pastor (p. 252)
deacon (p. 250)

Remember

- We belong to a parish.
- Many people serve our parish.
- Our parish worships together.
- Our parish cares for others.

OUR CATHOLIC LIFE

Caring for the Sick

Throughout history the Catholic Church has been a leader in caring for the sick. In the United States alone, there are almost six hundred Catholic hospitals.

Whenever we care for the sick, we show our respect for life. Our actions show that every human being has dignity because we are made in God's image. Catholic hospitals always try to protect human dignity—from the first moment of life to the last moment.

SHARING FAITH
with My Family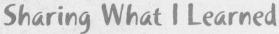

Sharing What I Learned

Look at the pictures below. Use each picture to tell your family what you learned in this chapter.

A Prayer for Our Parish

God, our Father, bless our parish. Help us to welcome all who come to worship.

Jesus, be with us as we celebrate your life, death, and Resurrection.

Holy Spirit, fill our parish with your love. Help us to love one another in our parish and in our family.

Amen.

The Church at Home

Your parish comes together to celebrate and pray. Your family can do this, too! Ask your family to set aside a time when everyone can be together. Plan a special meal. Make that time a celebration.

Share happy memories. Remember the gifts that God has given your family. Talk about the ways your family can help in your parish.

Refrigerator Prayer Card
(Pray this prayer with your family.)

Cut out this card. Place it where everyone can see it. Each time you see this card, pray the prayer again.

Visit Sadlier's
www.WeBelieveweb.com

 Connect to the Catechism
For adult background and reflection, see paragraphs 2179, 1348, 2182, and 2186.

God Calls Us to Holiness

12

WE GATHER

Leader: Let us listen to the word of God.

Reader: A reading from the first Letter of Saint John

"Beloved, if God so loved us, we also must love one another. No one has ever seen God. Yet, if we love one another, God remains in us, and his love is brought to perfection in us." (1 John 4:11, 12)

The word of the Lord.

All: Thanks be to God.

🎵 Only a Shadow

The love we have for you, O Lord,
Is only a shadow of your love for us;
Only a shadow of your love for us,
Your deep abiding love.

Our lives are in your hands,
Our lives are in your hands.
Our love for you will grow, O Lord;
Your light in us will shine.
Your light in us will shine
'Til we meet face to face.

What would you say if someone asked you, "What do you want to be when you grow up?"

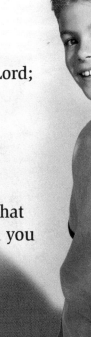

WE BELIEVE
God calls each of us.

In Baptism God calls all of us to love and to serve him. This is the mission we share as members of the Church. Our mission is to learn from Jesus and to continue his work in the world. We are called to show others who Jesus is so they will love and follow him, too.

A **vocation** is God's call to serve him in a certain way. Each baptized person has a vocation to love and serve God. There are specific ways to follow our vocation: the married life, the single life, the priesthood, and the religious life.

None of us lives our vocation alone. We live it as a member of the Church.

With a partner talk about people in your parish who follow their vocations to serve God. Give some examples of how they do this.

God calls everyone to be holy.

Most Catholics live out their vocation as laypeople. **Laypeople** are baptized members of the Church who share in the mission to bring the good news of Christ to the world.

Some laypeople are called to the vocation of married life. A husband and wife show Jesus to the world by the love that unites them. One important way they live out their vocations is by teaching their family to pray and to follow Jesus Christ.

Some laypeople live their vocation as single people in the world. They, too, answer God's call by living their lives as Jesus did. They use their time and talents to serve others.

Key Words

vocation (p. 253)

laypeople (p. 251)

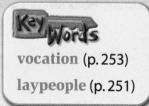

God calls all people to holiness. Our holiness comes from sharing God's life. To live a life of holiness means to share the good news of Jesus and help to build up God's Kingdom. We do this when we:

- tell others in our parish, our school, and our workplace about Jesus

- treat others as Jesus did

- care for those in need

- help others to know that God's life and love are alive in the world.

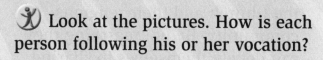

Look at the pictures. How is each person following his or her vocation?

Draw a way you follow God's call right now.

God calls some men to be priests.

Some men are called by God to serve as priests. When a man follows this call, he accepts a special ministry within the Church. In the sacrament of Holy Orders, he is ordained to the priesthood by a bishop.

Priests promise not to marry. This allows them to share God's love with all people and to go wherever the bishop sends them.

How have the priests in your parish helped you learn about Jesus?

Ask God to help them to continue their work in the Church.

God calls some people to religious life.

Some Church members follow Jesus Christ in the religious life. They are priests, brothers, or sisters who belong to religious communities. They share their lives with God and others in a special way.

As members of their religious communities they make **vows**, or promises to God. The vows usually are chastity, poverty, and obedience. Those in religious life promise to:

- live a life of loving service to the Church and their religious community. By not marrying they can devote themselves to sharing God's love with all people.

- live simply as Jesus did and own no personal property.

- promise to listen carefully to God's direction in their lives and to go wherever their religious community sends them to do God's work.

Those in religious life serve the Church in many different ways. Some live alone; others live in community. Some live apart from the world so they can pray all the time. Others combine prayer with a life of service as teachers, social workers, missionaries, doctors, and nurses.

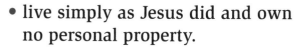
As Catholics...

A deacon is a man who is ordained in the sacrament of Holy Orders. A bishop ordains him as a special minister to the people. He lays his hands on the man and asks the Holy Spirit to strengthen him in preaching, baptizing, and serving the Church.

Does your parish have a deacon? What does he do in your parish?

vows (p. 253)

WE RESPOND

The Church needs the help and support of people in every vocation. Each vocation is important for the growth of the Church.

Write a prayer asking God to help all Church members in their vocations.

_____

_____

_____

_____

Write T if the sentence is true. Write F if the sentence is false.

1. A job is the invitation to serve God in the Church in a special way. _____

2. Laypeople are baptized members of the Church who share in the mission to bring the good news of Christ to the world. _____

3. Those in religious life make vows, or promises to God. _____

4. Bishops ordain priests through the sacrament of Confirmation. _____

Answer the questions.

5. What is a vocation? Why do we say that everyone in the Church has a vocation?

_____

_____

_____

ASSESSMENT

This week, read a Catholic newspaper or your parish bulletin. Find at least one person who is serving the Church. Write a short paragraph about this person. Tell what he or she is doing to follow Jesus and to help others grow in holiness.

We Respond in Faith

Reflect & Pray

In the Bible, God tells us, "I have called you by name: you are mine." (Isaiah 43:1) How does this make you feel? How can you convince others that they, too, are important to God?

Lord, you have called me by name. Help me to answer your call this week by

_____

_____

_____

Key Words

vocation (p. 253)
laypeople (p. 251)
vows (p. 253)

Remember

- God calls each of us.
- God calls everyone to be holy.
- God calls some men to be priests.
- God calls some people to religious life.

OUR CATHOLIC LIFE

Helping Poor People

The saints are examples of holiness. They show us how to follow Jesus. Martin de Porres was born in Lima, Peru, in 1579. During his childhood he was not always treated with respect. But he learned how to treat others with respect.

When he grew up, Martin became a religious brother. He spent each day caring for poor children and for the sick and homeless. We can follow Jesus with all our hearts as Saint Martin did.

SHARING FAITH with My Family

Sharing What I Learned

Look at the pictures below. Use each picture to tell your family what you learned in this chapter.

A Prayer for Those Who Help Us

God, thank you for the people who help us.

Thank you for our pope, bishops, and priests.

Thank you for our religious brothers and sisters.

Thank you for the married and single people who do so much for our Church.

Thank you especially for

_____.

We ask this in your name, Lord Jesus Christ. Amen.

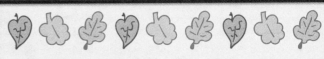

Family Vocations

With your family make a "Family Vocation Tree." Put the names of your parents, grandparents, uncles, and aunts on this tree. Find out how each person is serving God in the Church.

Refrigerator Prayer Card

(Pray this prayer with your family.)

Cut out this card. Place it where everyone can see it. Each time you see this card, pray the prayer again.

Visit Sadlier's
www.WeBelieveweb.com

Connect to the Catechism
For adult background and reflection, see paragraphs 1213, 825, 1719, 1565, and 915.

Advent

Advent   Christmas   Ordinary Time   Lent   Three Days   Easter   Ordinary Time

"Prepare the way of the Lord,
make straight his paths."

Luke 3:4

The season of Advent helps us prepare for the coming of the Son of God.

WE GATHER

🎵 **Prepare the Way**

Prepare the way
for the coming of God.
Make a straight path
for the coming of God.

WE BELIEVE

The word *Advent* means "coming." Each year during Advent we prepare to celebrate the first coming of the Son of God. We prepare to celebrate the birth of Jesus Christ at Christmas.

During Advent, we rejoice that Jesus is our Savior. He is the Son of God sent to save us from sin. We remember that God's people waited many, many years for the Savior to come. During those years of waiting, God spoke to his people through the prophets. The prophets told the people to prepare for the Savior.

The people were to:

- pray and worship God
- work for peace
- be just and fair to everyone
- turn away from sin and ask God for the help to live a good life.

The four weeks of Advent are a special time for us. Like God's people many years ago, we prepare for the coming of the Savior. We pray to God, seek his forgiveness, and work for peace. We wait and watch for the Son of God to come again. We prepare for the second coming of Jesus Christ.

 What can you do during Advent to prepare the way of the Lord? Write ways along this path.

WE RESPOND

The Church honors saints all year long. Here are some saints that we honor during Advent. They help us to rejoice in the coming of the Lord. Their lives help us to see that the Lord is near.

The people of Sweden were suffering from hunger. They prayed to Saint Lucy. They soon received help.

Mary made an appearance to a poor man who lived in Guadalupe, Mexico. We know him as Saint Juan Diego.

Saint Nicholas helped poor families by giving them money.

Talk about some things your family and parish do to celebrate the season of Advent.

✝ We Respond in Prayer

Leader: Rejoice in the Lord for he is near!

All: Rejoice in the Lord for he is near!

Reader: A reading from the Letter of Saint Paul to the Philippians

"Rejoice in the Lord always. I shall say it again: rejoice! Your kindness should be known to all. The Lord is near."
(Philippians 4:4–5)

The word of the Lord.

All: Thanks be to God.

🎵 Do Not Delay

Do not delay,
come, Lord, today:
show us the way
to the Father.

Do not delay,
come, Lord, today:
show us the way
to you.

SHARING FAITH with My Family

Sharing What I Learned

Look at the pictures below. Use each picture to tell your family what you have learned in this chapter.

Advent Gifts

To prepare to celebrate Christmas, encourage your family to give "gifts of kindness" to others. Cut out small squares from Christmas wrapping paper. Each square represents a gift of kindness. Then put a box next to the gift squares.

Invite each family member to do a kind act each day during Advent. Then ask each one to write that kind act on a gift square and place the square into the box. At Christmas put the box of gift squares under the tree as your family's gift to Jesus.

A Family Prayer for Advent

(Lead your family in this prayer.)

Lord Jesus, help us to make room for you in our hearts this Advent.

Come, Lord Jesus!

my kind act was to gi

Visit Sadlier's

www.WeBelieveweb.com

Connect to the Catechism
For adult background and reflection, see paragraph 524.

Christmas

"Today is born our Savior, Christ the Lord!"

Responsorial Psalm, Christmas Mass at Midnight

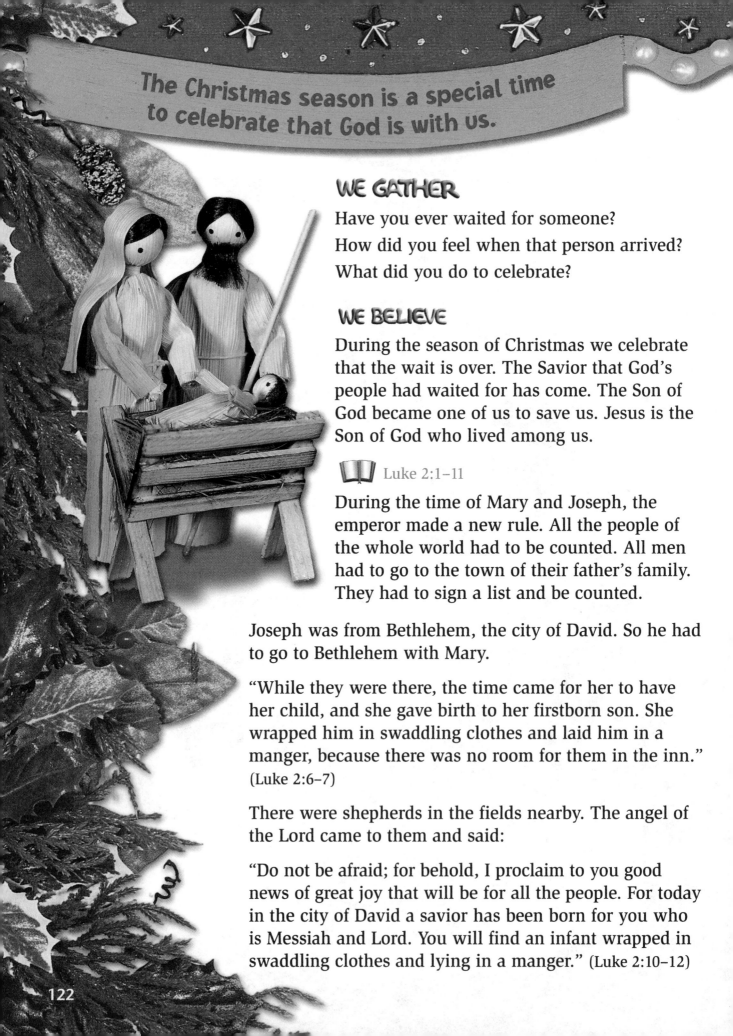

WE GATHER

Have you ever waited for someone?

How did you feel when that person arrived?

What did you do to celebrate?

WE BELIEVE

During the season of Christmas we celebrate that the wait is over. The Savior that God's people had waited for has come. The Son of God became one of us to save us. Jesus is the Son of God who lived among us.

Luke 2:1–11

During the time of Mary and Joseph, the emperor made a new rule. All the people of the whole world had to be counted. All men had to go to the town of their father's family. They had to sign a list and be counted.

Joseph was from Bethlehem, the city of David. So he had to go to Bethlehem with Mary.

"While they were there, the time came for her to have her child, and she gave birth to her firstborn son. She wrapped him in swaddling clothes and laid him in a manger, because there was no room for them in the inn." (Luke 2:6–7)

There were shepherds in the fields nearby. The angel of the Lord came to them and said:

"Do not be afraid; for behold, I proclaim to you good news of great joy that will be for all the people. For today in the city of David a savior has been born for you who is Messiah and Lord. You will find an infant wrapped in swaddling clothes and lying in a manger." (Luke 2:10–12)

Jesus is our Lord and Messiah. During Advent and Christmas we hear Jesus called Emmanuel. The name *Emmanuel* means "God with us." This is what we are celebrating during Christmas: God is with us today, now, and forever.

One way we share the joy of Christmas is through music. Write your own song to tell others the good news that Jesus is with us. Use a tune you know or make up one of your own.

_____

_____

_____

The Christmas season is a season of celebration. The Church celebrates many important feasts during this time.

December 25	Christmas
First Sunday after Christmas	Holy Family
Second Sunday after Christmas	Epiphany
Third Sunday after Christmas	The Baptism of the Lord
December 26	Saint Stephen
December 27	Saint John the Apostle
December 28	The Holy Innocents
December 29	Saint Thomas Becket
January 1	Mary, the Mother of God
January 4	Saint Elizabeth Ann Seton
January 5	Saint John Neumann

WE RESPOND

Draw one way your parish celebrates during the Christmas season.

✝ We Respond in Prayer

Leader: We thank you, God, for the lives of your holy people. Be with us as we ask their prayers for us.

All: Blessed be God for ever.

Reader: Saint Stephen was a deacon. He was the first to give his life for his faith in Jesus.

Saint Stephen,

All: Pray for us.

Reader: Jesus chose John to be an apostle. Saint John was the author of one of the four gospels. He wrote that God is love.

Saint John,

All: Pray for us.

Reader: King Herod did not want Jesus the Savior to live. He ordered all the baby boys two years of age and under to be killed! We call them the Holy Innocents. Their lives remind us of God's great gift of life.

Holy Innocents,

All: Pray for us.

Leader: Jesus shares God's gift of life with each of us. Praise God!

All: Blessed be God for ever.

CHRISTMAS

SHARING FAITH
with My Family

Sharing What I Learned

Look at the pictures. Use each picture to tell your family what you learned in this chapter.

Around the Table

Gather together each evening during the Christmas season. Share special things you did or received as part of your celebration of the season. For example, you might share songs, prayers, cards you received, or crafts you made.

Christmas Calendar

Make a calendar of the Christmas season. Mark Christmas Day and fill in the special names for the Sundays of the Christmas season.

Then fill in the names of the saints we remember during this season. Find out about their lives. Why do you think the Church honors them during Christmas?

Christmas Season

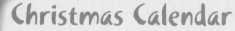

Visit Sadlier's

www.WeBelieveweb.com

Connect to the Catechism
For adult background and reflection, see paragraph 526.

**Match the words in Column A with the correct descriptions
in Column B.**

A	B
1. vocation	_____ promise to God
2. prayer	_____ listening and talking to God
3. Apostles' Creed	_____ the official public prayer of the Church
4. vow	_____ God's call to serve him in a certain way
5. liturgy	_____ Christian statement of beliefs

Write T if the sentence is true. Write F if the sentence is false.

6. _____ Catholic social teaching tells us that we have a responsibility to share the good things of the world.

7. _____ The bishops of the Church are the successors of the apostles.

8. _____ The Lord's Prayer is also called Our Prayer.

9. _____ One mark of the Church is that it is *catholic,* which means "universal."

10. _____ Priests, sisters, and brothers who belong to religious communities make vows of poverty, chastity, and justice.

Find ten words related to prayer in the puzzle. Use these words to tell your group about prayer.

```
B I N P G L I T N G I L
L T K R H T V H T R H I
E L U A L K R A B S L S
S I N I G I O N I L G T
S N L S S V L K R H G E
I N T E R C E S S I O N
N G L I T L I G L N D I
G L W O R S H I P Y L N
L R I V I N G V I N G G
I S O T A L K I N G O N
P E T I T I O N I O N I
L R L I T U R G Y L G Y
```

The Church Leads Us in Worship

UNIT 3 SHARING FAITH as a Family

What Media Violence Does to Kids

By age eighteen, American children have witnessed approximately 200,000 acts of violence on television alone. Add video games, movies, and music lyrics, and the number escalates dramatically. The impact on children is enormous. Here are just some of the reasons why parents and teachers need to be vigilant about children's exposure to media violence.

Violence in American media tends to be justified, that is, it is often carried out by the "good guy" against the "bad guy." Children quickly learn that this is an acceptable way to solve problems. This is hardly the message of the Gospel!

Most young children are unable to separate fantasy from reality. Thus, the computer graphics that make a movie dinosaur so life-like entertains adults while it terrifies children.

In the same manner, a child may see the repeated footage of a catastrophe on a news program as a new event each time. This raises their level of fear and anxiety to greater heights. Therefore, limit your child's exposure to graphic news footage. During times of national or local crises, they need reassurance. Talk to them honestly, and let them know that you are doing everything possible to make sure they are safe.

It is up to parents to teach children to love one another and to respect the precious gift of life.

What Your Child Will Learn in Unit 3

A presentation of the seven sacraments begins Unit 3. The children will be able to describe the sacraments of Christian Initiation (Baptism, Confirmation, Eucharist), the sacraments of Healing (Penance and Reconciliation, and Anointing of the Sick) and the sacraments at the Service of Communion (Matrimony and Holy Orders). The children will more fully realize that the Mass is the celebration of the Eucharist. The four parts of the Mass are then explained. These are the Introductory Rites, the Liturgy of the Word, the Liturgy of the Eucharist, and the Concluding Rites. The last two chapters of Unit 3 concentrate on the sacraments of healing: Penance and Reconciliation, and the Anointing of the Sick.

Plan & Preview

▶ Your child will be making a thank-you card to share with the entire family. Have a sheet of construction paper or drawing paper on hand. *(Chapter 16 Family Page)*

▶ You might want to obtain a photograph of someone special who has died in your family for use in the "Remembering Someone Special" activity. *(Chapter 19 Family Page)*

Note the Quote

"He who has courage and faith will never perish in misery."

Anne Frank

From the Catechism

"The family is the 'domestic church' where God's children learn to pray 'as the Church' and to persevere in prayer."

(Catechism of the Catholic Church, 2685)

Eucharistic Prayer

God of power and might,

we praise you through your Son, Jesus Christ,

who comes in your name.

He is the Word that brings salvation.

He is the hand you stretch out to sinners.

He is the way that leads to your peace.

God our Father,

we had wandered far from you,

but through your Son you have brought us back.

You gave him up to death

so that we might turn again to you

and find our way to one another.

(Eucharistic Prayer for Masses of Reconciliation II)

We Celebrate the Sacraments

15

WE GATHER

✝ **Leader:** God loves us very much. Let us thank God for all the ways he shows his love for us. Let us thank God for sending his Son.

Reader: "For God so loved the world that he gave his only Son, so that everyone who believes in him might not perish but might have eternal life." (John 3:16)

All: Thank you, God, for giving us your Son, Jesus. Amen.

🎵 Jesus Is with Us

Jesus is with us today,
beside us to guide us today.
Jesus teaches us, Jesus heals us,
for we are his Church;
we are his chosen;
we are the children of God.

☀ What are some signs that you see in your neighborhood? Tell why each one is important.

WE BELIEVE
The Church celebrates the sacraments.

Every day we can see all kinds of signs. A sign stands for or tells us about something. A sign can be something we see or something we do.

Jesus often pointed to ordinary things to help us to learn more about God. He spoke about birds, wheat, and even wildflowers as signs of God's love. Jesus' actions were signs of God's love, too. He held children in his arms. He touched people and healed them. He comforted sinners and forgave them.

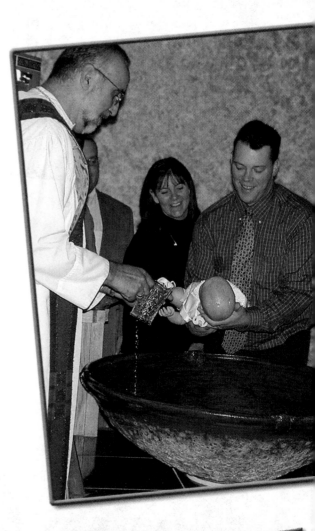

The Church celebrates seven special signs. We call these signs sacraments. A **sacrament** is a special sign given to us by Jesus through which we share in God's life and love. The seven sacraments are Baptism, Confirmation, Eucharist, Penance and Reconciliation, Anointing of the Sick, Holy Orders, and Matrimony.

Through the power of the Holy Spirit, we receive and celebrate God's own life and love in the sacraments. Our share in God's life and love is called **grace**. Through the power of grace, we grow in holiness. The sacraments help us to live as Jesus' disciples.

List the sacraments you have received.

_____

_____

_____

As Catholics...

Sacramentals are blessings, actions, and special objects given to us by the Church. They help us to respond to the grace we receive in the sacraments. Blessings of people, places, and food are sacramentals. Actions such as making the sign of the cross and the sprinkling of holy water are sacramentals. Some objects that are sacramentals are statues, medals, rosaries, candles, and crucifixes.

Name a sacramental that is part of your life at home.

Baptism, Confirmation, and Eucharist are the sacraments of Christian initiation.

We are joined to Jesus and the Church through the **sacraments of Christian initiation**: Baptism, Confirmation, and Eucharist. Another word for *initiation* is *beginning*. Through the sacraments of Christian initiation, a new life of grace begins in us.

In Baptism the Church welcomes us. We become children of God and members of the Church. Each of us is born with **original sin**, the first sin committed by the first human beings. Through Baptism God frees us from original sin and forgives any sins we may have committed. God fills us with grace, his life and love.

In Confirmation we are sealed with the Gift of the Holy Spirit. The Holy Spirit gives us strength and courage to live as disciples of Jesus.

In the Eucharist we praise and thank God the Father for sending his Son, Jesus. We receive Jesus' Body and Blood in Holy Communion. We grow closer to Jesus and all the members of the Church.

Key Words

sacrament (p. 253)

grace (p. 251)

sacraments of Christian initiation (p. 253)

original sin (p. 252)

In groups talk about how your parish celebrates the sacraments of Christian initiation.

Reconciliation and Anointing of the Sick are sacraments of healing.

During his ministry Jesus healed many people. Sometimes he did this when he cured them of their sicknesses. At other times Jesus forgave people their sins.

Jesus gave the Church the power to continue his healing work. The Church does this especially through two sacraments: Reconciliation and Anointing of the Sick. These sacraments are called sacraments of healing.

In the sacrament of Reconciliation, we confess our sins to the priest and promise to do better. In the name of God, the priest forgives our sins. Our relationship with God and others is healed.

In the sacrament of the Anointing of the Sick, the priest lays his hands on the sick. He blesses them with holy oil and prays for their health. They are strengthened in their faith and sometimes their bodies are healed. They receive the peace of Christ.

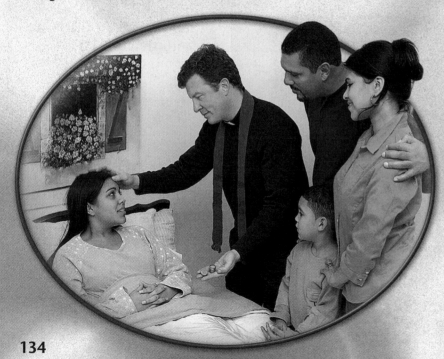

Think about someone you need to forgive or someone you know who is sick. What can you do to show them your love and care?

134

Holy Orders and Matrimony are sacraments of service to others.

Through Baptism God calls each one of us to be a sign of his love to others. We each have a vocation to serve God and the Church. The Church celebrates two sacraments that are special signs of service: Holy Orders and Matrimony.

In the sacrament of Holy Orders, certain men are ordained to serve the Church as deacons, priests, and bishops. This sacrament gives them the grace to live out their vocation of service in the Church.

Bishops serve the Church by leading a larger community of faith called a diocese. They lead their dioceses in service, teaching, prayer, and sacraments. Under their guidance, priests also carry on the ministry of Jesus.

Priests usually serve in parishes. They lead the celebration of the sacraments, guide the people they serve, and reach out to those who are in need. Some priests teach in schools.

Along with the bishop and priests, deacons are ordained to serve their dioceses. Deacons do many things to help in their parish worship. They also have a special responsibility to serve those who are in need.

In the sacrament of Matrimony, or Marriage, the love of a man and woman is blessed. They are united in the love of Christ. The husband and wife receive the grace to help them to be faithful to each other. The sacrament also helps the couple to share God's love with their family. They grow in holiness as they serve the Church together.

WE RESPOND

👤 Draw or write how you and your friends join in the celebration of the sacraments.

Use the words in the box to complete the sentences.

Matrimony	Anointing of the Sick	sacrament
Reconciliation	Eucharist	

1. A _____ is a special sign given to us by Jesus through which we share in God's life and love.

2. Baptism, Confirmation, and _____ are the sacraments of Christian initiation.

3. Anointing of the Sick and _____ are sacraments of healing.

4. Holy Orders and _____ are sacraments of service to others.

Finish this sentence.

5. Through the sacraments _____

_____

_____

ASSESSMENT

Make a booklet of the sacraments you have celebrated. Describe each sacrament. Include drawings that show the celebration of the sacrament. Decorate the cover of your book.

We Respond in Faith

Reflect & Pray

What are some of the ways God shares his life and love with us?

_____

Jesus, help me to be a sign of God's love in today's world. Help me to

_____

Key Words

sacrament (p. 253)
grace (p. 251)
sacraments of Christian initiation (p. 253)
original sin (p. 252)

Remember

- The Church celebrates the sacraments.
- Baptism, Confirmation, and Eucharist are the sacraments of Christian initiation.
- Reconciliation and Anointing of the Sick are sacraments of healing.
- Holy Orders and Matrimony are sacraments of service to others.

Our Catholic Life

Martyrs for the Faith

In 1980 four American Catholic women, Sister Ita Ford, M.M., Sister Maura Clarke, M.M., Sister Dorothy Kazel, O.S.U., and Jean Donovan were killed in El Salvador. These women died as they had lived, serving God and the Church.

A *martyr* is someone who dies for his or her faith. Christian martyrs give their lives as a sign of God's love to others. Many martyrs have already been declared saints by the Church. Some day these four women may be officially declared saints, too.

SHARING FAITH
with My Family

Sharing What I Learned

Look at the pictures below. Use each picture to tell your family what you learned in this chapter.

BAPTISM

CONFIRMATION

Sacrament Reminders

Color the pictures for each sacrament. Cut out each one.
Collect all seven! With your family, choose one way to display
your sacrament reminders.

Visit Sadlier's

www.WE BELIEVE.web.com

 Connect to the Catechism
For adult background and reflection, see
paragraphs 1113, 1212, 1421, and 1534.

Celebrating Eucharist: The Mass

16

WE GATHER

✝ **Leader:** Everything good that we have is God's gift to us. Think quietly about what God has given you.

Reader: "Give thanks to the LORD, who is good, whose love endures forever."
(Psalm 106:1)

All: We thank you, O God!

Reader: "You are my God, I give you thanks; my God, I offer you praise."
(Psalm 118:28)

All: We thank you, O God!

☀ Many people celebrate special times with special meals. When have you and your family done this? What made the celebration special for you?

WE BELIEVE

Jesus celebrated Passover and the Last Supper.

Throughout their history, Jewish people have celebrated important events with special meals. On the feast of Passover, the Jewish people celebrate their freedom from slavery in Egypt. They remember that God "passed over" the houses of his people, saving them. They remember that God protected them from the suffering that came to Egypt.

On the night before he died, Jesus celebrated the Passover meal with his disciples in a new way. This meal that Jesus celebrated is called the Last Supper.

 Matthew 26:26–28

While Jesus and his disciples ate, Jesus took bread and blessed it. He then broke it and gave it to his disciples saying, "Take and eat; this is my body." (Matthew 26:26) Then Jesus took a cup of wine and gave thanks. He gave the cup to his disciples saying, "Drink from it, all of you, for this is my blood." (Matthew 26:27, 28)

At the Last Supper Jesus told his disciples to bless and break bread in his memory. He gave us the Eucharist. The Eucharist is the sacrament of Jesus' Body and Blood. At each celebration of the Eucharist, the Church follows Jesus' command to "Do this in memory of me." (Luke 22:19)

The word *eucharist* means "to give thanks." At the celebration of the Eucharist, the Church gives thanks for all that God gives us.

 Write what you can thank God for at the celebration of the Eucharist.

_____

_____

The Mass is a sacrifice and a meal.

The greatest gift God has given to us is his Son, Jesus. Jesus' greatest gift is giving up his life for us. The Church remembers Jesus' death and Resurrection at the Eucharist.

The celebration of the Eucharist is also called the Mass. The Mass is a sacrifice. A sacrifice is a gift offered to God by a priest in the name of all the people. Jesus offered the greatest sacrifice of all–his own body and blood on the cross. By his sacrifice Jesus reconciles us with God and saves us from sin.

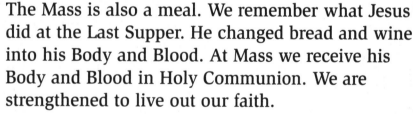

Key Words

Passover (p. 252)

Eucharist (p. 251)

Mass (p. 252)

sacrifice (p. 253)

The Mass is also a meal. We remember what Jesus did at the Last Supper. He changed bread and wine into his Body and Blood. At Mass we receive his Body and Blood in Holy Communion. We are strengthened to live out our faith.

What could you tell a younger child about what the Mass is? Act it out with a partner.

We take part in the Mass.

The Mass is a celebration. It is the Church's great prayer of thanksgiving and praise. It is important that each of us participate in the celebration.

We gather as the assembly. The **assembly** is the people gathered to worship in the name of Jesus Christ.

We can all:

- pray the responses
- sing praise to God
- listen to the readings and the homily
- pray for needs of the community
- offer the sign of peace to others
- receive Holy Communion.

The priest who leads us at the Mass is called the *celebrant*. Many parishes have deacons who serve at the Mass. Greeters and ushers welcome us and help us to find seats. During the Mass they collect our donations. Altar servers help the priest before, during, and after Mass.

Key Word

assembly (p. 250)

As Catholics...

Altar servers are men, women, boys, and girls who serve at the altar. They light the altar candles. They lead the entrance procession at the beginning of Mass. They may help the priest and deacon receive the gifts of bread and wine. They lead everyone out of church at the end of Mass.

Find out how boys and girls can become altar servers.

The musicians and choir lead us in singing. The reader proclaims passages from Scripture. Members of the assembly present the gifts of bread and wine. Special ministers of the Eucharist can help the priest give us Holy Communion.

How do you take part in the Mass? Talk about ways you can encourage others to participate in Mass.

We celebrate Mass each week.

Sunday is our great holy day. It is the day on which Jesus Christ rose from the dead. The Resurrection of Jesus took place on "the first day of the week." (Matthew 28:1)

In our parishes we come together at Mass each Sunday or Saturday evening. We give praise and thanks to God. Celebrating the Eucharist together is the center of Catholic life. That is why the Church requires all Catholics to take part in the weekly celebration of the Mass. We are also required to participate in Mass on special feasts called *holy days of obligation*.

There are many other important feast days in the Church. One of these is the feast of Our Lady of Guadalupe, which we celebrate on December 12. On these feasts and on every day of the year, we can take part in the Eucharist.

WE RESPOND

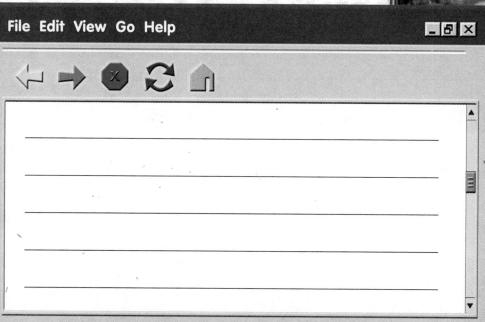 Send a message inviting people in your parish to take part in the Mass.

Holy Days of Obligation

· **Solemnity of Mary, Mother of God**
(January 1)

Ascension
(when celebrated on Thursday during the Easter season)

Assumption of Mary
(August 15)

All Saints' Day
(November 1)

Immaculate Conception
(December 8)

Christmas
(December 25)

File Edit View Go Help

Write the answer to each question.

1. What Jewish feast did Jesus celebrate at the Last Supper?

_____

2. What do we call the sacrament of the Body and Blood of Christ?

_____

3. The Mass is a meal. What else is it?

_____

4. What do we call the people gathered to worship in the name of Jesus Christ?

_____

5. Why do Catholics celebrate Mass each Sunday or Saturday evening?

_____

_____

_____

The feature story for a magazine is "The Eucharist: Why Is It Important?" What would you write in this story? What pictures would you use?

We Respond in Faith

Reflect & Pray

Jesus is present to us at Mass. What does this mean to you?

_____

_____

Jesus, I believe that you are with us when we come together in your name. This week, at Mass, help me

_____

_____

Key Words

Passover (p. 252)
Eucharist (p. 251)
Mass (p. 252)
sacrifice (p. 253)
assembly (p. 250)

Remember

- Jesus celebrated Passover and the Last Supper.
- The Mass is a sacrifice and a meal.
- We take part in the Mass.
- We celebrate Mass each week.

OUR CATHOLIC LIFE

Our Contributions Count

Catholics have always given money for the needs of the Church and the poor. At Mass our donations are collected during the preparation of the gifts. The money collected helps the parish meet its needs. It also is used to help others in need: for example, those who are sick or those who are victims of earthquakes, fires, or floods.

When you put your own donations in the basket at Mass, remember—your contribution counts. You are following Jesus by sharing what you have with others.

SHARING FAITH
with My Family

Sharing What I Learned

Look at the pictures below. Use each picture to tell
your family what you learned in this chapter.

Giving Thanks

Think about someone who has helped
your family. Send that person a thank-
you card. Take a sheet of paper. Fold
it in half; then fold it in half again.
Decorate the cover of the card. Invite
each member of your family to write a
note of thanks on the inside and sign
the card.

EUCHARIST

Sacrament Reminders

Color this picture for the sacrament of the
Eucharist. Cut it out. Keep it in a special
place. You should now have three
sacrament reminders. Collect all seven!

Visit Sadlier's

www.WeBelieveweb.com

Connect to the Catechism
For adult background and reflection, see
paragraphs 1340, 1323, 1348, and 1343.

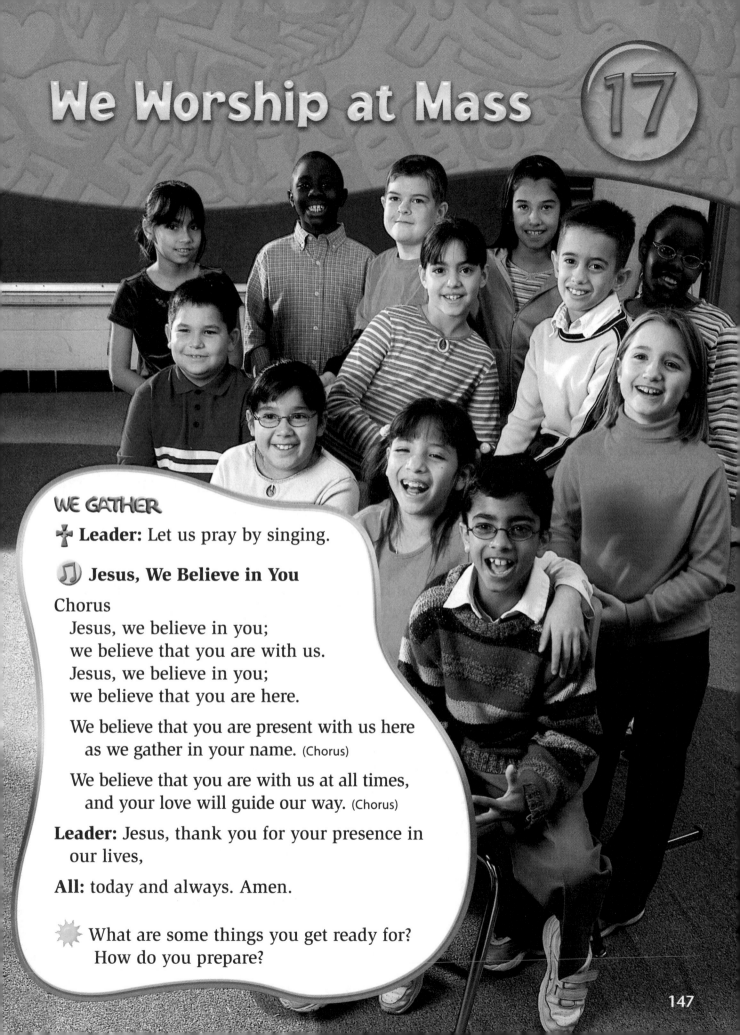

WE GATHER

✠ **Leader:** Let us pray by singing.

🎵 **Jesus, We Believe in You**

Chorus
> Jesus, we believe in you;
> we believe that you are with us.
> Jesus, we believe in you;
> we believe that you are here.

We believe that you are present with us here
as we gather in your name. (Chorus)

We believe that you are with us at all times,
and your love will guide our way. (Chorus)

Leader: Jesus, thank you for your presence in
our lives,

All: today and always. Amen.

☀ What are some things you get ready for?
How do you prepare?

Introductory Rites (p. 251)
Liturgy of the Word (p. 252)

WE BELIEVE

We gather to praise God.

The first part of the Mass is called the Introductory Rites. In the Introductory Rites we become one as we prepare to listen to God's word and to celebrate the Eucharist.

We gather together as members of the Church, the Body of Christ. We sing an opening song of praise to God. Then the priest welcomes us as God's people. With the priest we make the sign of the cross. The priest reminds us that Jesus is present among us.

The priest invites us to remember that we need God's forgiveness. We think about the times that we might have sinned. We tell God that we are sorry and ask for forgiveness.

On most Sundays of the year, we sing or say the "Gloria." We praise and bless God for his great love and care. This hymn of praise begins with: "Glory to God in the highest."

Think about your parish's celebration of the Mass last week. With a partner talk about what happened in the Introductory Rites.

We listen to God's word.

The Liturgy of the Word is the part of the Mass when we listen and respond to God's word.

On Sundays and other special days, there are three readings from Scripture. The first reading is usually from the Old Testament. After this reading we sing or say a psalm from the Old Testament. Then the second reading is from the New Testament. The readers end the first and second readings with: "The word of the Lord." We respond: "Thanks be to God."

The third reading is from one of the four gospels: Matthew, Mark, Luke, or John. The gospel reading is very special. We hear about the life and teachings of Jesus.

Before the gospel reading we show we are ready to hear the good news of Jesus Christ. We do this by standing and singing the Alleluia. The deacon or priest then proclaims the gospel. To proclaim the gospel means to announce the good news with praise and glory. At the end of the gospel the deacon or priest says: "The Gospel of the Lord."

We respond: "Praise to you, Lord Jesus Christ."

After the gospel reading, the priest or deacon gives the homily. The homily helps us to understand what the three readings mean in our lives. Then we all stand and state our belief in God by saying the creed.

In the *prayer of the faithful*, also called the *general intercessions*, we pray for our Church and our world. We ask God to help our leaders, our family and friends, all those who are sick and in need, and all those who have died.

Who would you like to pray for at Mass this week? Write a prayer for them here.

_____

_____

_____

_____

_____

We receive Jesus Christ.

During the **Liturgy of the Eucharist** the bread and wine become the Body and Blood of Christ, which we receive in Holy Communion. The altar is prepared for this part of the Mass. Members of the assembly bring forward our gifts of bread and wine and our gifts for the Church and the poor.

The priest then asks God to bless and accept the gifts we will offer. We also offer our whole lives to God. Now the *eucharistic prayer* begins. It is the great prayer of praise and thanksgiving. The priest prays this prayer in our name to the Father through Jesus Christ. Through this prayer we are united with Christ.

The priest recalls all that God has done for us. We sing a song that begins: "Holy, holy, holy Lord."

The priest then says and does what Jesus said and did at the Last Supper. Through these words and actions of the priest, by the power of the Holy Spirit, the bread and wine become the Body and Blood of Christ. This part of the eucharistic prayer is called the *consecration*. Jesus is truly present in the Eucharist. This is called the *real presence*.

At the end of the eucharistic prayer, we say or sing "Amen." Together we are saying "Yes, we believe."

Next we pray together the Lord's Prayer, the Our Father. We offer one another a sign of peace to one another. The priest then breaks the Bread while the "Lamb of God" prayer is sung.

Then we all come forward to receive Holy Communion. We sing as we go to receive to show our unity with one another. After communion we all sit in silence.

In groups talk about ways we can show that we are united to Christ and one another.

We go out to love and serve the Lord.

As the Mass ends we are encouraged to share the good news of Jesus with others. The last part of the Mass is the Concluding Rites. The **Concluding Rites** remind us to continue praising and serving God each day.

The priest says a final prayer thanking God for the Eucharist we have celebrated. He blesses us, and we make the sign of the cross. Then the priest or deacon, in Jesus' name, sends us out into the world. He says, "Go in peace to love and serve the Lord." We answer, "Thanks be to God."

We leave the church singing. With the help of the Holy Spirit, we try to help people who are in need. We do what we can to make our world a more loving and peaceful place. We try to treat others as Jesus would.

As Catholics...

After Holy Communion, the remaining consecrated Bread, or Hosts, are put in a special place in the church called the *tabernacle*. The Eucharist in the tabernacle is known as the *Blessed Sacrament*. The Blessed Sacrament can be taken to people who are dying and to those who are sick.

Jesus Christ is truly present in the Blessed Sacrament. Catholics honor Jesus' real presence by praying before the Blessed Sacrament.

The next time you are in church, kneel and pray to Jesus in the Blessed Sacrament.

WE RESPOND

 How could we love and serve others in these situations? Write your ideas.

• A family member is really tired.

We could:

_____

• A classmate is being "picked on."

We could:

_____

Key Words

Liturgy of the Eucharist (p. 252)

Concluding Rites (p. 250)

Write T if the sentence is true. Write F if the sentence is false.

1. The first part of the Mass is called the Introductory Rites. _____

2. We learn about the life and teachings of Jesus in the gospel reading. _____

3. The Liturgy of the Eucharist gets us ready to listen to God's word. _____

4. The Concluding Rites remind us to continue to praise God and to serve God and his people each day. _____

Answer the question.

5. How do we live out the Mass all through the week?

_____

_____

_____

_____

Make a poster to show what happens in each part of the Mass. Include the people who are involved. Write some of the responses said during Mass.

We Respond in Faith

Reflect & Pray

At the end of Mass, we are sent out to love and serve. What does this mean to you?

_____

_____

Complete this prayer.

Jesus, I believe in you and

_____

_____

Key Words

Introductory Rites (p. 251)

Liturgy of the Word (p. 252)

Liturgy of the Eucharist (p. 252)

Concluding Rites (p. 250)

Remember

- We gather to praise God.
- We listen to God's word.
- We receive Jesus Christ.
- We go out to love and serve the Lord.

OUR CATHOLIC LIFE

Saint Katharine Drexel

Katharine Drexel decided to use her inheritance to help others. She worked for the equal rights of Native Americans and African Americans.

In 1891, Katharine started a religious community called the Sisters of the Blessed Sacrament. She believed strongly that Jesus invites all people to join the Church and to take part in the Eucharist. Because of the efforts of Katharine and her sisters, many Native Americans and African Americans are active members of the Church today.

SHARING FAITH
with My Family

Sharing What I Learned

Look at the pictures below. Use each picture to tell your family what you learned in this chapter.

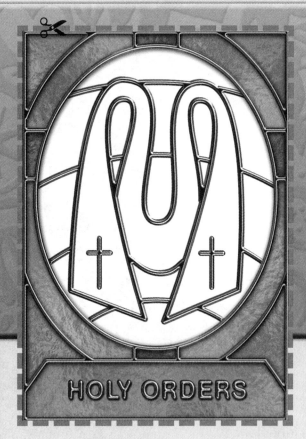

HOLY ORDERS

MATRIMONY

Sacrament Reminders

Color the pictures for each sacrament. Cut out each one. Collect all seven!

Visit Sadlier's

www.WeBelieveweb.com

Connect to the Catechism
For adult background and reflection, see paragraphs 1359, 1349, 1355, and 1694.

WE GATHER

✟ **Leader:** Sit quietly. Think about the last few days. Sometimes our actions and words do not show love. How have you acted with your family and friends? Let us pray an act of contrition together.

All: My God,
I am sorry for my sins with all my heart.
In choosing to do wrong
and failing to do good,
I have sinned against you
whom I should love above all things.
I firmly intend, with your help,
to do penance,
to sin no more,
and to avoid whatever
leads me to sin.
Our Savior Jesus Christ
suffered and died for us.
In his name, my God, have mercy.

☀ Think about an important choice you had to make. What did you think about before choosing? How did you know whether you made the right choice?

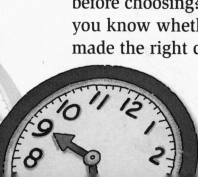

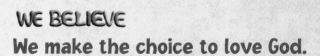

WE BELIEVE
We make the choice to love God.

God wants us to love him, ourselves, and others. This is God's law. When we live by the Ten Commandments and follow Jesus' example we obey God's law.

However, there are times we do not live the way Jesus wants us to live. We freely choose to do what we know is wrong. We commit a sin. **Sin** is a thought, word, or action that is against God's law. Sin is always a choice. That is why mistakes and accidents are not sins.

Some sins are very serious. These serious sins are mortal sins. A *mortal sin* is:

- very seriously wrong

- known to be wrong

- freely chosen.

People who commit mortal sin turn away completely from God's love. They choose to break their friendship with God. They lose the gift of grace, their share in God's life and love.

Not all sins are mortal sins. Sins that are less serious are *venial sins*. People who commit venial sins hurt their friendship with God. Yet they still share in God's life and love.

 Write one way you can show that you have chosen to love God today.

_____

_____

God is our forgiving Father.

Jesus told this story to help us to understand God's love and forgiveness.

📖 Luke 15:11–32

A rich man had two sons. One son wanted his share of the father's money. He wanted to leave home and have some fun. His father was sad, but he let his son have the money.

The son went away and began to spend his money. He used his money on all kinds of things. Soon all his money was gone.

The son found himself poor, dirty, hungry, and without friends. He thought about his father and his home. He decided to go home and tell his father that he was sorry.

When the father saw his son, he was so happy. The father rushed out and hugged him. The son said, "Father, I have sinned against heaven and against you; I no longer deserve to be called your son." (Luke 15:21)

But the father wanted everyone to know his son had come home. The father shouted to his servants, "Let us celebrate with a feast." (Luke 15:23)

Jesus told this story to show that God is our loving father. He is always ready to forgive us when we are sorry.

We receive God's forgiveness through the Church. Our relationship with God and the Church is made strong through the sacrament of Reconciliation.

🏃 Talk about times people forgive each other.

Key Word

sin (p. 253)

The sacrament of Reconciliation has several parts.

Examining our conscience is the first step in preparing for the sacrament of Reconciliation. Our **conscience** is God's gift that helps us know right from wrong.

When we examine our conscience, we ask ourselves whether or not we have loved God, others, and ourselves. We think about the things we have done and whether they were right or wrong. This examination of conscience helps us to know and to be sorry for our sins.

Contrition, confession, penance, and absolution are always part of the sacrament of Reconciliation.

Contrition is being sorry for our sins and firmly intending not to sin again. *Confession* is telling our sins to the priest. The priest may talk to us about the way we can love God and others.

A *penance* is a prayer or action that shows we are sorry for our sins. Accepting the penance shows that we are willing to change the way that we live. *Absolution* is God's forgiveness of our sins through the actions and words of the priest. The priest extends his hand and forgives us. He ends by saying,

"Through the ministry of the Church may God give you pardon and peace, and I absolve you from your sins in the name of the Father, and of the Son, † and of the Holy Spirit."

Write one reason why the Church celebrates the sacrament of Reconciliation.

• contrition •

• confession •

Key Word

conscience (p. 250)

conscience (p. 250)

As Catholics...

Many parishes have a separate space for celebrating the sacrament of Reconciliation. This is a special place where you meet the priest for individual confession and absolution. You can choose how you want to talk with the priest. You can sit and talk to him face-to-face or kneel behind a screen.

In your parish, where do you celebrate the sacrament of Reconciliation?

The Church celebrates the sacrament of Reconciliation.

The sacrament of Reconciliation is a celebration of God's love and forgiveness. Here are two ways the Church celebrates the sacrament of Reconciliation.

• penance •

Celebrating with the Community

We sing an opening hymn and the priest greets us and prays an opening prayer.

We listen to a reading from the Bible and a homily.

We examine our conscience and pray an act of contrition. We pray the Our Father.

I meet individually with the priest and confess my sins. The priest talks to me about loving God and others. He gives me a penance.

The priest extends his hand and gives me absolution.

After everyone has met with the priest, we join together to conclude the celebration. The priest blesses us, and we go in the peace and joy of Christ.

Celebrating Individually

The priest greets me. I make the sign of the cross.

The priest or I may read something from the Bible.

I meet individually with the priest and confess my sins. The priest talks to me about loving God and others. He gives me a penance.

I pray an act of contrition.

The priest extends his hand and gives me absolution.

Together the priest and I give thanks to God for his forgiveness.

WE RESPOND

How can you thank God for his forgiveness after celebrating the sacrament of Reconciliation?

• absolution •

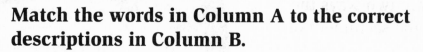

Review

Grade 3
Chapter 18

Match the words in Column A to the correct descriptions in Column B.

A   B

1. sin   _____ telling our sins to a priest

2. contrition   _____ being sorry for our sins and
                               intending not to sin again

3. penance   _____ freely choose to do what we
                               know is wrong

4. confession   _____ something we do to show we are
                               sorry for our sins

Answer the question.

5. In the sacrament of Reconciliation, how do we receive
   absolution?

   _____

   _____

   _____

   _____

ASSESSMENT

Design an invitation for your parish Web site or
parish bulletin. Invite parish members to a
Reconciliation service. Be sure to tell them how
important it is to celebrate this sacrament together.

We Respond in Faith

Reflect & Pray

There are many choices that I have to make in my life. How do the choices that I make show my love for God and others?

_____

_____

Jesus, your forgiveness helps me

_____

_____

Key Words

sin (p. 253)
conscience (p. 250)

Remember

- We make the choice to love God.
- God is our forgiving Father.
- The sacrament of Reconciliation has several parts.
- The Church celebrates the sacrament of Reconciliation.

OUR CATHOLIC LIFE

An Example of Forgiveness

In 1980, Pope John Paul II wrote a letter to the whole Church. This letter reminded people that God is merciful and forgiving. Six months later, the pope was nearly killed when Mehmet Ali Agca shot him. Although Pope John Paul II was seriously wounded, he publicly forgave Agca. Later the pope visited with his attacker in prison. The pope personally forgave the man who had tried to kill him. The pope's willingness to forgive is an example to all of us. We are called to forgive those who hurt us.

Sharing What I Learned

Look at the pictures below. Use each picture to tell your family what you learned in this chapter.

Family "I Am Sorry" Card

Encourage your family to say, "I am sorry." On an index card print "I am sorry." On the other side, print "Please forgive me." Decorate the card and put it in a special place. When you need to ask forgiveness of a family member, give that person this card to help you say you are sorry.

RECONCILIATION

Sacrament Reminders

Color the picture for the sacrament of Reconciliation. This is your sixth sacrament reminder card. Cut it out. Collect all seven!

Visit Sadlier's

www.WeBelieveweb.com

Connect to the Catechism
For adult background and reflection, see paragraphs 1428, 1439, 1450–1460, and 1469.

We Pray for Healing and Eternal Life

19

WE GATHER

✝ **Leader:** Jesus asked people to believe in him. He healed those who had faith in him. Let us rejoice and sing this song:

🎵 **Walking Up to Jesus**

So many people in the house with
 Jesus,
People, people, people come to see
 him!

Jesus looked, and said to the man
 who could not walk:
"Get up now. You are healed.
 You can walk!
And all at once the man jumped up
 and everyone said, "OH!"

For he was walking in the house
 with Jesus,
Walking, walking,
 walking up to Jesus!

☀ Think of a time when you felt hurt
 or sick. Who helped you? How did
 you feel after they helped you?

WE BELIEVE

Jesus cared for and healed the sick.

Jesus cared for all people. When those who were sick, hungry, poor, or in need reached out to him, Jesus comforted them. Sometimes he cured them of their illnesses. He gave them a reason to hope in God's love and care.

📖 Mark 10:46–52

Jesus was leaving a town with his disciples and a large crowd. A blind man named Bartimaeus was sitting by the side of the road. He called out to Jesus to have pity on him. People in the crowd told Bartimaeus to be quiet. But he kept calling out to Jesus anyway.

"Jesus stopped and said, 'Call him.' So they called the blind man, saying to him, 'Take courage; get up, he is calling you.' He threw aside his cloak, sprang up, and came to Jesus. Jesus said to him in reply, 'What do you want me to do for you?'

The blind man replied to him, 'Master, I want to see.' Jesus told him, 'Go your way; your faith has saved you.' Immediately he received his sight and followed him on the way." (Mark 10:49–52)

🤸 Act out this gospel story.

Jesus listened to people who needed his help. Jesus often visited the homes of people who were sick. Wherever he went people asked Jesus to help and to heal them.

Jesus wants us to have his comfort and peace, too. No matter what our needs are Jesus gives us hope and the joy of his love.

The Church heals us in Jesus' name.

Today the Church carries on Jesus' healing work. One of the most important ways is in the sacrament of the Anointing of the Sick. Through the sacrament those who are sick receive God's grace and comfort. The Holy Spirit helps them to trust in God's love. The Holy Spirit helps them to remember that God is always with them.

Any Catholic who is seriously ill may receive the Anointing of the Sick. Those in danger of death, for example, or those about to have a major operation are encouraged to celebrate this sacrament.

During this sacrament a priest uses the oil of the sick. The oil of the sick is holy oil that has been blessed by the bishop for use in the Anointing of the Sick.

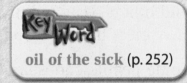

Key Word

oil of the sick (p. 252)

A priest anoints the forehead of each sick person with this oil, saying:

"Through this holy anointing may the Lord in his love and mercy help you with the grace of the Holy Spirit."

The Anointing of the Sick is a sacrament for the whole Church. Family and parish members join with those who are sick in celebrating this sacrament.

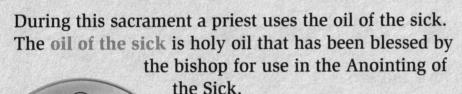

At this sacrament we all pray that God will heal the sick. We also remember our own call to follow Jesus by loving and caring for people who are sick.

With a partner talk about some times people may need Jesus' comfort and hope. Write one way we can help them.

_____

_____

We believe in eternal life with God.

Sometimes people may be so sick that they do not get better. We pray that they will not feel lonely and sad. We pray that they will trust in Jesus' promise to be with them always. Jesus will be with them at their death as he was during their life.

Death is not easy for us to understand or to accept. As Christians we do not see death as the end of life. We believe that our life continues after death, in a different way. We call this eternal life. **Eternal life** is living forever with God in the happiness of heaven.

When people choose to love and serve God and others, they will live with God forever. Heaven is life with God forever.

Some people choose not to love and serve God. Some people choose to break their friendship with God completely. Because of this choice, they separate themselves from God forever. Hell is being separated from God forever.

God does not want anyone to be separated from him. Yet many people who die in God's friendship may not be ready to enter the happiness of heaven. We believe these people enter into purgatory, which prepares them for heaven. Our prayers and good works can help these people so they may one day be with God in heaven.

Name some ways that the choices we make show God that we are his friends.

166

The Church celebrates eternal life with God.

No one can take away the sadness that we feel when someone we love dies. Even though we are sad, Catholics trust that this person will enjoy eternal life.

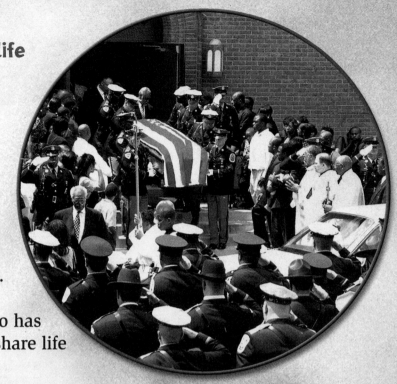

At a special Mass we thank God for the life of the person who has died. This Mass is called a **funeral Mass**. We gather as the Church with the family and friends of the person who has died. We pray that this person will share life with God forever.

The funeral Mass gives us hope. We are reminded that:

- at Baptism we were joined to Christ
- Jesus died and rose from the dead to bring us new life
- death can be the beginning of eternal life.

At the funeral Mass we pray that the person who has died will be joined to Christ in heaven. We celebrate our belief that everyone who has died in Christ will live with him forever. We give comfort to the person's family and friends by spending time and praying with them.

WE RESPOND

Design a card for someone who might need comfort and hope.

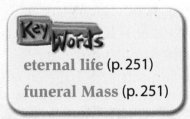

eternal life (p. 251)

funeral Mass (p. 251)

Fill in the blanks.

1. The Church continues Jesus' healing in the sacrament of the _____.

2. In the sacrament of the Anointing of the Sick, the priest anoints a sick person with _____.

3. _____ is living forever with God in the happiness of heaven.

4. A _____ is a special Mass at which we thank God for the life of a person who has died.

Answer the question.

5. What is one way the funeral Mass reminds us of our Baptism?

_____

_____

_____

_____

ASSESSMENT

Imagine you are a television news reporter. Write a news story to be shown on your local television station. In your news story describe what your parish can do to care for those who are sick and dying.

We Respond in Faith

Reflect & Pray

The Church brings Jesus' healing, comfort and hope to those who need it. What do you think this means?

_____

_____

Loving God, where there is sadness, help me to

_____

_____

Key Words

oil of the sick (p. 252)
eternal life (p. 251)
funeral Mass (p. 251)

Remember

- Jesus cared for and healed the sick.
- The Church heals us in Jesus' name.
- We believe in eternal life with God.
- The Church celebrates eternal life with God.

OUR CATHOLIC LIFE

Pastoral Care for the Sick

By Baptism, Catholics are called to be concerned about others. Following the example of Jesus, we show respect for all people. In each of our parishes, help is provided to the sick, the elderly, and the dying. Priests, deacons, and special ministers of the Eucharist visit these people. They read from the Bible and pray together. Holy Communion is also offered during the visit. You can help by praying for those who are sick. You can also show your care by sending cards, by visiting, or by phoning. Remembering the sick in these special ways lets them know they are not forgotten.

SHARING FAITH
with My Family

Sharing What I Learned

Look at the pictures below. Use each picture to tell
your family what you learned in this chapter.

Remembering and Sharing

Invite your family to remember someone
special who has died. This person now
lives forever with God. Place a picture
of the person on the table and tell
stories about him or her. Remember
things that this person especially
enjoyed. Together as a family, pray
for this person.

ANOINTING
OF THE SICK

Sacrament Reminders

Color the picture for the sacrament of
Anointing of the Sick. Cut it out. This
is your last sacrament reminder card.
You should now have all seven cards!

Visit Sadlier's

www.WeBelieveweb.com

Connect to the Catechism
For adult background and reflection, see
paragraphs 1503, 1511, 1681, and 1684.

Lent

20

"Come to me heedfully,
listen, that you may have life."

Isaiah 55:3

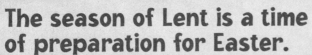

The season of Lent is a time of preparation for Easter.

WE GATHER

Have you had to take the time to get ready for a special event like a family get-together?

How did you prepare?

What did you do?

WE BELIEVE

Lent is our time of preparation for Easter. All during Lent, we remember three very important things:

- We belong to God through Baptism.
- We live now by grace, the life of God within us.
- We will live forever with God because Jesus died and rose to bring us God's life.

The season of Lent lasts forty days. It begins on Ash Wednesday. On this day we are marked with blessed ashes. The ashes are used to make a cross on our foreheads. The ashes are a sign that we are sorry for our sins and that we look forward to life with God forever.

♫ Ashes

We rise again from ashes,
from the good we've failed to do.
We rise again from ashes,
to create ourselves anew.
If all our world is ashes,
then must our lives be true,
an offering of ashes,
an offering to you.

172

Lent is a special time for the Church. It is a special time to renew our Baptism. We remember the waters of Baptism that cleansed us from sin and brought us new life. We recall that in Baptism we were joined to Jesus and first received a share in God's life, grace. This is the grace we also receive in the Eucharist and the other sacraments.

Celebrating the sacraments of Reconciliation and the Eucharist is an important part of the season of Lent. The sacraments bring us into the wonder of Christ's death and Resurrection. We are strengthened by God's love and forgiveness. We are nourished by the Body and Blood of Christ.

Lent is a time to grow in faith. We think and pray about the life we have because Jesus died and rose for us. We think about what we believe as Christians. We pray with those who will celebrate the sacraments of initiation at the Easter Vigil.

During Lent we make a special effort to follow Jesus. We do this through prayer, penance, and acts of love and mercy. Doing these things during Lent helps us to renew our Baptism and gets us ready for the great Three Days.

Caring For Our Community
Catholic Diocese of Gary
and
Northwest Indiana Habitat for Humanity

OPERATION RICE BOWL
Catholic Relief Services

WE RESPOND

Talk together with your class about what you can do to grow in faith and love during Lent. Write some of the ideas suggested.

_____

_____

_____

_____

Look back at what you have written. Put a check beside the things you would like to do.

✝ We Respond in Prayer

Leader: O merciful God, you loved us so much you sent your Son to bring us life. Help us to believe in and follow him.

All: We believe!

Reader: A reading from the Gospel of John

"For God so loved the world that he gave his only Son, so that everyone who believes in him might not perish but have eternal life. For God did not send his Son into the world to condemn the world, but that the world might be saved through him." (John 3:16–17)

The Gospel of the Lord.

All: Praise to you, Lord Jesus Christ.

🎵 **Ashes**

Thanks be to the Father,
who made us like himself.
Thanks be to his Son,
who saved us by his death.
Thanks be to the Spirit
who creates the world anew
From an offering of ashes,
an offering to you.

SHARING FAITH
with My Family

Sharing What I Learned

Look at the pictures below. Use each picture to tell your family what you learned in this chapter.

Prayers for Lent

Set up a special place for your family to pray together during this season of Lent. Display a cross or crucifix and photos of family baptismal celebrations in your prayer space.

Pray together one of these prayers during each week of Lent.

Week 1: Lord, help us live by your word.

Week 2: Lord Jesus, Son of God, have mercy on us.

Week 3: Lord, give us hearts full of love.

Week 4: Here we are, Lord. We come to do your will.

Week 5: Lord, grant us your peace.

Week 6: Jesus, thank you for all you have done for us.

 Connect to the Catechism
For adult background and reflection, see paragraph 540.

The Three Days

"Most blessed of all nights,
chosen by God
to see Christ rising from the dead!"

Exsultet, Easter Vigil

The Three Days celebrate that Jesus passed from death to new life.

WE GATHER

When have you celebrated a long weekend or holiday with your family?

What did you do or say that made it a special time to be with your family?

WE BELIEVE

The Three Days are the Church's greatest celebration. They are like a bridge. The Three Days take us from the season of Lent to the season of Easter.

Adoration before the Blessed Sacrament, Holy Thursday night

During the Three Days, we gather with our parish. We celebrate at night and during the day. The Three Days are counted from evening to evening. The first day starts on the evening of Holy Thursday. We remember what happened at the Last Supper. We celebrate that Jesus gave himself to us in the Eucharist. We remember the ways Jesus served others. We have a special collection for those who are in need.

On Good Friday, we remember the suffering and death of Jesus on the cross. In church, the altar is completely bare. We listen to the Bible readings that tell us about Jesus' death. We give special honor to the cross, and we praise God for the life that comes from Jesus' death. We pray for the whole world. Then we wait and pray.

Reading of the Passion, Good Friday

Easter candle lit by Easter fire, Easter Vigil

On Holy Saturday, we think about all that happened to Jesus. We pray that we might be joined to Jesus. We gather again as a community at night for the Easter Vigil. A fire is burning bright. The Easter candle is lit and we sing "Christ our light!"

We listen to many different stories from the Bible. We remember all the great things God has done for us. We sing with joy to celebrate that Jesus rose from the dead.

New members of the Church receive the new life of Christ in Baptism, Confirmation, and the Eucharist. We rejoice with them. This is the most important and the most beautiful night of the year! Holy Saturday turns into Easter Sunday.

On Easter Sunday, we listen to the story of Jesus' Resurrection. We receive the Body and Blood of the risen Jesus in Holy Communion. We are given new strength and joy to live his risen new life. Alleluia!

WE RESPOND

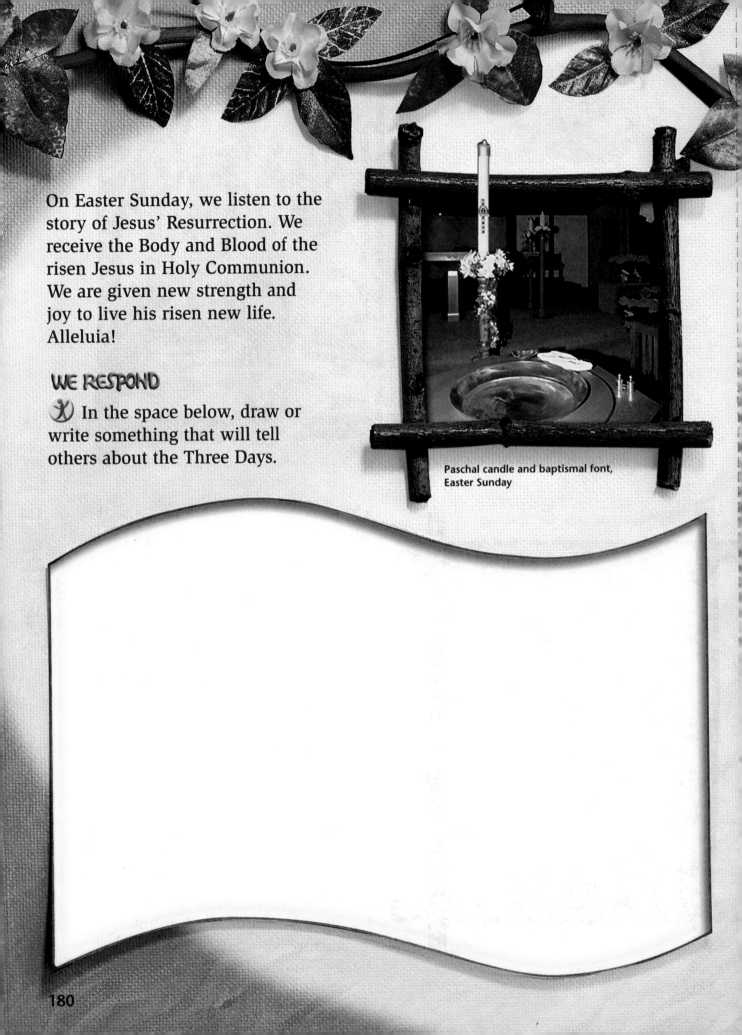 In the space below, draw or write something that will tell others about the Three Days.

Paschal candle and baptismal font, Easter Sunday

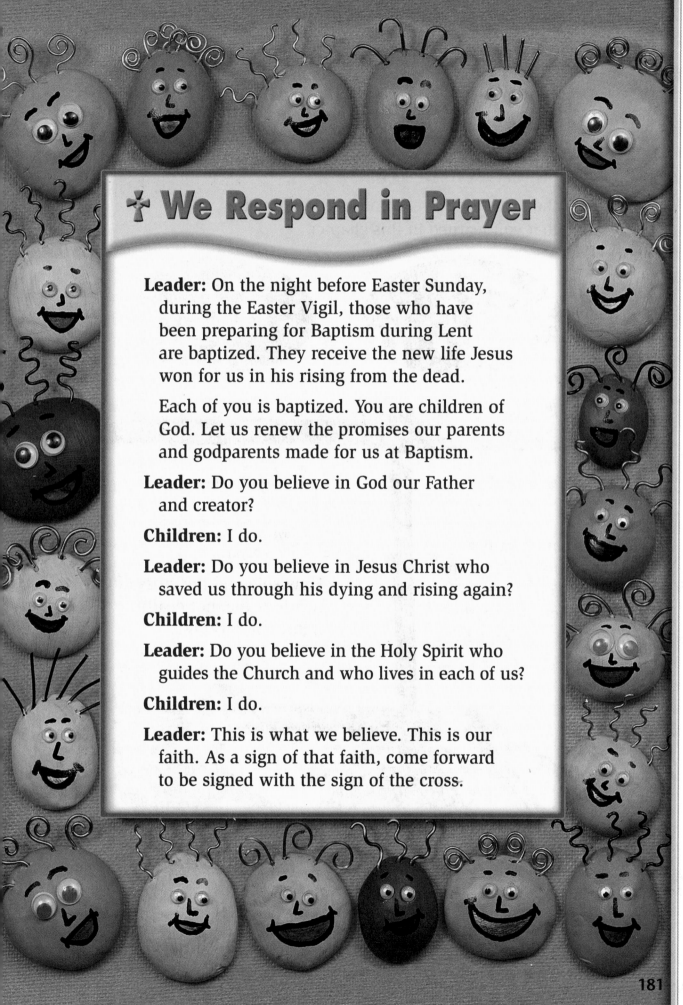

✝ We Respond in Prayer

Leader: On the night before Easter Sunday, during the Easter Vigil, those who have been preparing for Baptism during Lent are baptized. They receive the new life Jesus won for us in his rising from the dead.

Each of you is baptized. You are children of God. Let us renew the promises our parents and godparents made for us at Baptism.

Leader: Do you believe in God our Father and creator?

Children: I do.

Leader: Do you believe in Jesus Christ who saved us through his dying and rising again?

Children: I do.

Leader: Do you believe in the Holy Spirit who guides the Church and who lives in each of us?

Children: I do.

Leader: This is what we believe. This is our faith. As a sign of that faith, come forward to be signed with the sign of the cross.

SHARING FAITH
with My Family

Sharing What I Learned

Look at the pictures. Use each picture to tell your family what you learned in this chapter.

A Three Day Cross

Invite your family to decorate a cross for the Three Days. Include decorations that reflect the faith and hope in your family.

A Family Prayer for the Three Days

(Pray this prayer with your family during the Three Days.)

How splendid the cross of Christ!
It brings life, not death;
light, not darkness.

Theodore of Studios

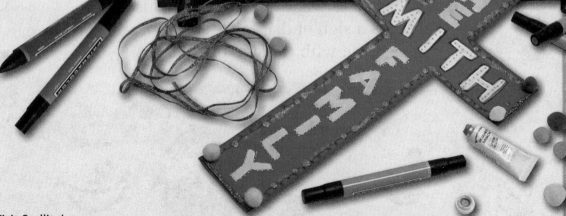

Visit Sadlier's

www.WE BELIEVE.web.com

Connect to the Catechism
For adult background and reflection, see paragraph 647.

Use the words in the box to complete the sentences.

sacrifice	healing	initiation
Anointing	Mass	absolution

1. Baptism, Confirmation, and the Eucharist are sacraments of

Christian _____.

2. By his _____ Jesus reconciles us with God and saves us
from sin.

3. The celebration of the Eucharist is also called the _____.

4. God's forgiveness of our sins through the actions and words of the

priest is called _____.

5. Through the sacrament of the _____ of the Sick, those
who are sick are strengthened by the Holy Spirit.

Answer these questions in the space provided.

6. How can a husband and wife who have been united in the sacrament
of Matrimony live out their vocation of service in the Church?

_____

_____

7. How can a priest live out his vocation of service in the Church?

_____

_____

The pictures show two of the four parts of the Mass.

Label the part shown in each picture and write a short description of it on the lines.

_____

_____

_____

_____

_____

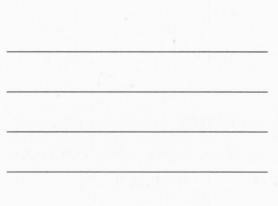

_____

_____

_____

_____

_____

Choose one of these projects.

- Make a poster illustrating the seven sacraments.

- Imagine that your neighbor's good friend has just died. Write a letter of comfort to your neighbor.

We Are Called to Discipleship

UNIT 4 SHARING FAITH as a Family

Five Ways to Manage Conflict in the Home

Few homes are free from the presence of conflict. It is a part of learning how to relate to one another. Suppressing conflict can often add fuel to the fire. Here are five ways to manage conflict in the home so that it doesn't get out of hand.

1. Teach children to name their anger or hurt without accusing others. The use of "I" messages ("I feel," "I think") is an effective way to do this.

2. Parenthood does not equate with being a referee. Encourage your children to work out disagreements on their own. Agree to mediate only as a last resort.

3. Stick to the point. Arguments get out of hand when past hurts and unresolved issues get thrown into the fray. Stay focused on solving the *current* source of conflict.

4. Don't repeat second or third-hand information. Relating what Grandma or Cousin Bob thinks of another person's actions is rarely helpful. Repeating someone else's words can make the situation more complicated.

5. Pick your battles. Let's face it—some things aren't worth the time and energy it takes to fight about them. Let go of insignificant issues, especially ones held onto out of pride or needing to be "right."

What Your Child Will Learn in Unit 4

Unit 4 challenges the children to appreciate and accept that we, as the followers of Jesus Christ, are all called to discipleship. In order to understand how we can live as disciples, the children will appreciate that the Church respects all people and religions. They will also discover that the Church is present throughout the world. This leads to a clear and comprehensive explanation of the Latin (or Roman) and Eastern Rites of the Catholic Church. To have the children continue to grasp the meaning of discipleship, the saints are presented as examples of holiness. No such discussion is complete without presenting Mary, the Mother of God. The children will learn ways they can honor Mary. Unit 4 concludes with an inspiring explanation of the Kingdom of God and how the Church and each one of us as its members can help the Kingdom of God to grow every day.

Plan & Preview

▶ You might want to have available pieces or cardboard or stiff paper as well as a glue stick in order to make the trading cards that appear on each *Family Page* throughout the unit.

Captain Timothy Stackpole

A Story in Faith

Timothy Stackpole

It was one of those days in New York City that makes postcards. It was a great day to have off from work. Tim Stackpole certainly thought so. Tim had a way of enjoying a day and making others around him do the same. This morning it was his turn to teach Confirmation class at his local parish.

From the Catechism

"Becoming a disciple of Jesus means accepting the invitation to belong to *God's family,* to live in conformity with His way of life."
(*Catechism of the Catholic Church,* 2233)

So it was a surprise, a terrible shock, to hear the heart-stopping news that swept New York that September 11th morning.

Tim was a firefighter. He loved being a firefighter. Tim was one of the best. Six months before, Tim had fought his way back to active service after being badly burned in a major fire. Most people thought it would be impossible for Tim to return to the fire department he loved. "Impossible" was not in the vocabulary of Timothy Stackpole.

Now, Tim was rushing to the burning World Trade Center. Terrorists had aimed two hijacked planes into each of the Twin Towers' gleaming facades. Both were on fire. Both were filled with innocent people. Both needed the help and courage of firefighters like Timothy Stackpole.

Tim died there, giving his life to help others. There are many definitions for hero. Being called to be a disciple of Jesus Christ can take numerous forms. But on that burning day in September, Timothy Stackpole was the living example of both a courageous hero and a faithful disciple.

We Continue the Work of Jesus

WE GATHER

✝ **Leader:** Imagine that you are with the apostles. Jesus has just been crucified. You are praying together in a room.

(Pause)

All of a sudden, Jesus is standing in the room with you. He says,

Reader 1: "Peace be with you."
(John 20:19)

Leader: Think about the way you feel seeing Jesus again.
(Pause)

Now Jesus looks at you and says,

Reader 2: "As the Father has sent me, so I send you." (John 20:21)

Leader: What do you think Jesus means? Where is he sending you?
(Pause)

Let us pray together:

All: Jesus, we are listening to the message you have for each of us. You are sending us out to share the good news that you have saved us. Help us as we go out to share your love with others. Amen.

☀ Tell about a time when you were given something important to do. How did doing this help you, your family, or your friends?

WE BELIEVE

Jesus brings God's life and love to all people.

Jesus, the Son of God, had very important work to do. His mission was to bring God's life and love to all people.

 Luke 4:16–19

Jesus began his work among the people after he was baptized by his cousin John. In the synagogue in Nazareth, Jesus read these words from the prophet Isaiah.

"The Spirit of the Lord is upon me,
　because he has anointed me
　　to bring glad tidings to the poor.
He has sent me to proclaim liberty to captives
　and recovery of the sight to the blind,
　　to let the oppressed go free,
and to proclaim a year acceptable to
　the Lord." (Luke 4:18–19)

Jesus then went to many towns and villages telling people that God cared for and loved them. Jesus showed those who were poor or lonely that they were important. He healed people who were sick. He stood up for those who were treated unjustly. Jesus cared for the people's needs and taught his disciples to do the same.

Jesus offered others the peace and freedom that come from God's love and forgiveness. He shared God's love with them, and they believed.

Jesus asks his disciples to care for the needs of others. Name one way you can do this.

Jesus shares his mission with his disciples.

Jesus gave his apostles a mission. Jesus asked the apostles to go to all nations and teach people about him. The apostles were to baptize all those who believed in him.

The Holy Spirit strengthened and guided the apostles. The apostles led the other disciples in doing the work of Jesus. This is the good news they shared:

- God made all people in his image.

- God loves and cares for everyone.

- God so loved the world that he sent his only Son who showed us how to live and saved us from sin.

- Jesus taught us to love God above all else and to love our neighbors as ourselves.

- Jesus worked for justice and peace and he asks all of us to do the same.

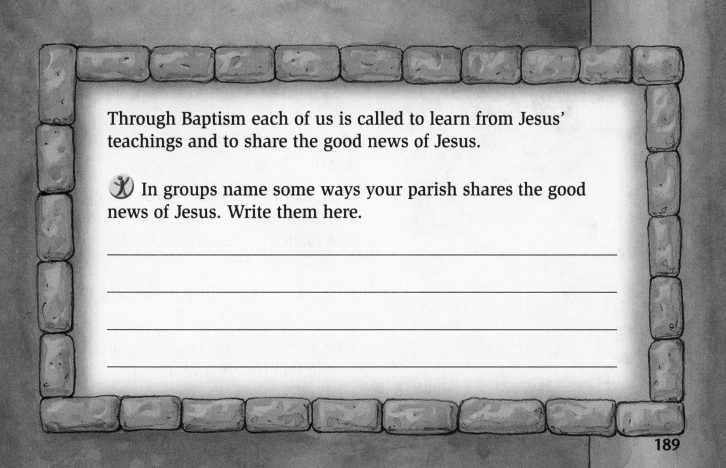

Through Baptism each of us is called to learn from Jesus' teachings and to share the good news of Jesus.

In groups name some ways your parish shares the good news of Jesus. Write them here.

_____

_____

_____

_____

The Church works for justice and peace.

Jesus taught that all people are created and loved by God. We are all made in God's image. So all people deserve to be treated fairly and with respect. Making sure this happens is one way the Church works for justice and peace in the world.

The pope and bishops teach us about the need to protect human life. In many ways they remind us to respect the rights of all people.

Our parishes serve those in need and work together to build better communities. In our families, schools, and neighborhoods, we live out Jesus' command to love others as he loves us.

The whole Church works for justice. We help to protect children, to care for the poor, and to welcome people who are new to our country.

With a partner come up with a slogan to remind your class about the need for justice and peace.

We live out the good news of Jesus Christ.

As disciples of Jesus we are called to live out the good news and to work for peace and justice as Jesus did. To show we are disciples we can:

• love and obey our parents and those who care for us

• be a friend to others, especially those who feel lonely and left out

• help those who are treated unfairly

- treat everyone fairly and with respect
- learn about and care for people who need our help in this country and in the world.

As disciples of Jesus we do not work alone. Together with other Church members, we can visit those who are sick or elderly. We can volunteer in soup kitchens or homeless shelters. We can help those who have disabilities. We can help those from other countries to find homes and jobs and to learn the language. We can write to the leaders of our state and country. We can ask our leaders for laws that protect children and those in need.

WE RESPOND

 Draw one way your family can bring Jesus' love to others.

As Catholics...

Both at home and in other countries, missionaries help to do the work of Jesus. They may be ordained priests and deacons, religious sisters and brothers, and single or married laypeople. Some missionaries serve as teachers, nurses, doctors, or social workers.

Some people spend their whole lives being missionaries. Others spend a month, a summer, or even a year or two doing missionary work.

Find out about some missionaries in your neighborhood.

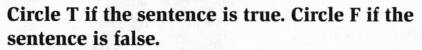

Circle T if the sentence is true. Circle F if the sentence is false.

1. We show we are disciples only when we participate in Mass.

    T   F

2. Jesus asks his disciples to continue his work.

    T   F

3. Only the pope and bishops share the good news and work for justice.

    T   F

4. Only some people deserve to be treated fairly and with respect.

    T   F

Answer the questions.

5. What was Jesus' mission? How did he carry it out?

_____

_____

_____

ASSESSMENT

Prepare a talk for children your age. Tell how you can work with others for justice and peace.

We Respond in Faith

Reflect & Pray

The way I can serve others is

_____

_____

Jesus, you gave your disciples a mission.
Help me to

_____

_____

Remember

- Jesus brings God's life and love to all people.
- Jesus shares his mission with his disciples.
- The Church works for justice and peace.
- We live out the good news of Jesus Christ.

OUR CATHOLIC LIFE

Supporting Missionary Work

The Catholic Church Extension Society helps missionary work in the United States. It began in 1905. It receives many donations. The money that it donates goes to people and places that need it the most. In a recent year, seventy-four dioceses in thirty-four states received donations from the Catholic Church Extension Society.

SHARING FAITH
with My Family

Sharing What I Learned

Look at the pictures below. Use each picture to tell your family what you learned in this chapter.

We Believe Trading Cards

Ask your family to help you design a **Helping the Kingdom Grow** trading card. Attach a photo or draw an image of a family member on the front. Complete the faith facts about this person on the back.

Disciple of the Day

Invite your family to talk about people who continue the work of Jesus and ways they do this.

Helping the Kingdom Grow

FOLD ON THIS LINE

Name _____

My favorite time and place to pray is

_____.

My favorite story about Jesus is

_____.

I will help our parish by

_____.

Visit Sadlier's

www.WeBelieve.web.com

Connect to the Catechism
For adult background and reflection, see paragraphs 543, 551, 2419, and 2449.

The Church Respects All People

23

WE GATHER

✝ **Leader:** Let us sit quietly.
Thank God for his many blessings.
Now let us offer our prayers to him.

Reader: Let us pray
for all our brothers and sisters
who share our faith in Jesus Christ,
that God may gather and keep together
in one Church
all those who seek the truth
with sincerity.
We pray to the Lord.

All: Lord hear our prayer.

Reader: Let us pray
for the Jewish people,
the first to hear the word of God,
that they may continue to grow
in the love of his name
and in faithfulness to his covenant.
We pray to the Lord.

All: Lord hear our prayer.

Leader: Almighty and eternal God,
enable those who do not
acknowledge Christ
to find the truth as they walk before you
in sincerity of heart.
We ask this through Christ our Lord.

All: Amen.

What interesting things have you learned
about people and places in other countries?
Talk about these things together.

WE BELIEVE

People around the world have different beliefs about God.

Christians are people of faith who believe in and follow Jesus Christ. Not everyone in the world believes in Jesus as Christians do. This does not mean that they are not people of faith. They believe in God and worship God in different ways. They live their faith at home, in school, and in their communities.

Jews are people of faith who keep God's law and follow the Ten Commandments. They often call God Yahweh and Lord. They celebrate many feasts and holidays.

Christians have a special connection to the Jewish people. Many Christian beliefs and practices come from the Jewish faith.

Muslims are people of faith who follow the teachings of Muhammad. They call God Allah. They pray and worship God in unique ways. Muslims have some of the same beliefs as Jews and Christians.

Many native tribes worship God by honoring and respecting his creation. They call God the Great Spirit.

There are many other people of faith. They, too, follow a set of beliefs and show their faith in different ways.

🧍 Look at the pictures on these pages. Are any of these faiths practiced in your town or city? Talk about ways you can show respect for people of all faiths.

Native American boy at powwow

Buddhist woman offering incense

Hindu festival

The Jewish faith is important to Christians.

Reading the Old Testament can help us to understand Jewish history and beliefs. This is important because they are part of our history, too.

We learn from the Old Testament about God's covenant with Moses. A **covenant** is an agreement between God and his people.

In this covenant with Moses and the people, God promised to be their God. He would give his people a land all their own. The people promised to be God's people and to believe in him. They promised to worship only the one true God. They agreed to live by God's law and to follow the Ten Commandments.

God continued to love his people. He spoke to them through the prophets. The prophets reminded the people of their promises to God.

John the Baptist was one of these prophets. He prepared the people for the coming of the Messiah. The Messiah would be sent by God to bring mercy, peace, and justice.

Some Jews believed that Jesus was this Messiah. They followed him and became his disciples. After Jesus' death and Resurrection, the number of Jesus' disciples grew. Those who followed Jesus and his teachings became known as Christians.

Muslims at prayer

Jewish Passover meal

covenant (p. 250)

In this scroll, write a prayer for God's blessings on our Jewish brothers and sisters.

_____

_____

_____

Christ calls his followers to be united.

At the Last Supper, Jesus prayed that his followers would always be one community. He prayed, "I pray not only for them, but also for those who will believe in me through their word, so that they may all be one . . ." (John 17:20–21)

Christians believe in and follow Jesus. Catholics are Christians. As Catholics we follow the teachings and example of Jesus Christ. We belong to the Catholic Church.

There are Orthodox Christians and Episcopal Christians. Other Christians may be Lutheran, Methodist, Presbyterian, and Baptist.

All Christians have some important things in common. All Christians are baptized and share some very important beliefs.

- God is Father, Son, and Holy Spirit.

- Jesus is both divine and human.

- Jesus died for our sins and rose again from the dead.

- The Bible was inspired by the Holy Spirit.

Today the Catholic Church is working with other Christians to bring together all baptized people. This work toward Christian unity is called **ecumenism**.

In groups list some things we can do to show that we are Christians. Share your ideas.

The Church works for Christian unity.

How can each one of us work for Christian unity? We first need to know our faith and be the best Catholics we can be. Other Christians can learn about the Catholic Church by who we are and what we do.

As Catholics...

Each year in January the Church celebrates a week of prayer for Christian Unity. We pray that all Christians may be one. Prayer services and discussion groups are held. Together Christians try to grow in love and understanding. As Catholics every week at Mass we pray that all Christians will be one.

Find out how your parish works with other Christian churches in your neighborhood.

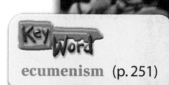

Key Word

ecumenism (p. 251)

We try to treat people the way Jesus did. We receive the sacraments. Receiving the sacraments is an important part of being Catholic. The sacraments strengthen our faith. The sacraments help us grow closer to God and to one another.

We also need to know our faith so we can share it with others. We cannot tell other people what it means to be a Catholic if we do not know. We read the Bible and ask God to help us to understand his word. We learn the history of our Church. We also learn what the Church teaches about important topics. This helps us to follow the Church's teachings.

WE RESPOND

What is something you can do to show you are Christian?

Draw or write something that will encourage all Christians to work together for unity.

Match the words in Column A to the correct descriptions in Column B.

A	B
1. Muslims	_____ call God *Yahweh* and *Lord*
2. Jews	_____ an agreement between God and his people
3. covenant	_____ believe in and follow the teachings of Jesus Christ
4. Christians	_____ call God *Allah*

Answer the questions.

5. What is ecumenism? Why is it important?

_____

_____

_____

_____

Find out about a religion other than Christianity. Visit your local library and/or use the Internet. Then write a report on your findings.

We Respond in Faith

Reflect & Pray

It is not always easy to respect people who believe and worship differently than we do.

I can be more respectful by

_____

_____

Complete this prayer:

Jesus, you showed us how to treat others.

This week, help me to _____

_____

Key Words

covenant (p. 250)
ecumenism (p. 251)

Remember

- People around the world have different beliefs about God.
- The Jewish faith is important to Christians.
- Christ calls his followers to be united.
- The Church works for Christian unity.

OUR CATHOLIC LIFE

Houses of Worship

Most people gather to pray together in houses of worship. Some of these places have special names. Hindus, Buddhists, and Jews gather to worship in buildings called *temples*. Jews also gather for prayer and study in buildings called *synagogues*. The buildings that Muslims worship in are called *mosques*. Christians, including Catholics, have several names for their houses of worship—*church*, *chapel*, and *cathedral* are a few of them. We respect the rights of all people to worship. So we respect their holy places, too.

SHARING FAITH
with My Family

Sharing What I Learned

Look at the pictures below. Use each picture to tell your family what you learned in this chapter.

We Believe Trading Cards

Ask your family to help you design a **Helping the Kingdom Grow** trading card. Attach a photo or draw an image of a family member on the front. Complete the faith facts about this person on the back.

We Respect All People

Talk about ways that your family can show respect for families of different faiths.

Helping the Kingdom Grow

FOLD ON THIS LINE

Name _____

My favorite time and place to pray is

_____.

My favorite story about Jesus is

_____.

I will show my respect for people of different faiths by

_____.

Visit Sadlier's
www.WeBelieveweb.com

Connect to the Catechism
For adult background and reflection, see paragraphs 843, 839, 838, and 855.

202

The Church Is Worldwide

24

Buena nueva

La bonne nouvelle

WE GATHER

✝ **Leader:** Let us gather quietly to listen to the word of God.

Reader: A reading from the holy Gospel according to Luke

"He said to them, 'To the other towns also I must proclaim the good news of the kingdom of God, because for this purpose I have been sent.'" (Luke 4:42–43)

The Gospel of the Lord.

All: Praise to you, Lord Jesus Christ.

🎵 **We Are the Church**

Chorus
We are the Church,
 happy to be the children
 in God's family.

We are the Church,
 happy to be the children
 in God's family.

We are sharing the Good News.
We are sharing the Good News.
Ev'ryone old and young.
Ev'ryone weak and strong.

We are sharing the Good News,
 for (Chorus)

Il lieto messagio

Good News

☀ Do any of your family, friends, and neighbors come from another country? What do you know about that country?

203

WE BELIEVE
The Catholic Church is all over the world.

The Catholic Church is made up of people from all over the world. They have different customs. Customs are the way a group of people live, dress, and celebrate. The customs and history of each part of the world add beauty and wonder to the Church.

All around the world Catholics use their local customs to praise and worship God. In Africa drums and tribal dances are part of the celebration of the Mass. In Asia the Catholic Church celebrates with special traditions. For example, in Korea and in the Philippines musical instruments and native costumes add to the celebration of the Mass.

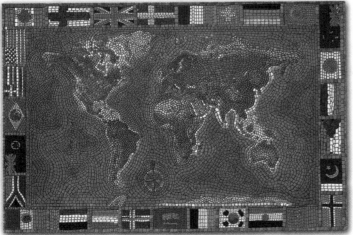

Many Catholics in the United States follow the customs of their native countries. For example, many Mexican Americans keep the custom of using luminarias. *Luminarias*, also called *faroles*, are paper sacks filled with sand and lighted candles. Before evening Masses luminarias are placed on paths leading to the church.

The Catholic Church is a wonderful mix of people with different languages, music, and customs. We are united by our faith in Jesus and our membership in the Church. We can all grow and learn from the traditions of one another.

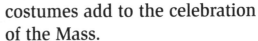
Immaculate Conception Church

If you could worship with Catholics in any part of the world, where would you choose to go? Why?

Catholics share the same faith.

Catholics in different parts of the world sometimes celebrate their Catholic faith in different ways. A **Rite** is a special way that Catholics celebrate, live, and pray to God.

Most Catholics in the United States follow the Latin, or Roman, Rite. Other Catholics follow one of the Eastern Rites.

Catholics of the Eastern Rites and Latin Rite make up the whole Catholic Church. We are all joined together in three important ways.

- We all share the same beliefs. We state these beliefs in creeds such as the Apostles' Creed.

- We all celebrate the seven sacraments.

- With our bishops we are all united with the pope as one Church.

Catholics everywhere live as disciples of Jesus in their families, schools, and communities.

Think about Catholics in your neighborhood or city. Write one way they practice their faith.

_____

_____

As Catholics...

All Catholics are officially listed as members of the Catholic Church. In the parish where you were baptized, your name is written down in a special book called the *Baptismal Register*. Your name will always be there. As you celebrate other sacraments, they are also recorded in the Baptismal Register.

Find out the names of the parishes where your family members were baptized.

Key Word

Rite (p. 253)

Saint Michael's Russian Catholic Church

205

Catholics celebrate their faith in different ways.

Catholics celebrate and live out their faith in many ways. For example, all Catholics participate in the liturgy, the official public prayer of the Church.

However, the different Rites have different ways of celebrating. In the liturgy, the wording of some of the prayers is not always the same. The things the priest and people do are a little different, too.

The pictures on these pages show ways the Eastern Rites and the Latin Rite celebrate their Catholic faith. Talk about what the people in these pictures are doing. What is familiar to you? What questions might you have for the people in these pictures?

Receiving the Eucharist

Talk about ways your parish celebrates its faith. Then act one way out.

The altar at Curé of Ars Church

We are the light of the world.

As Catholics, we are united as one community. We are joined with Catholics all around the world. We pray and grow in holiness. No matter how we celebrate, we are all disciples of Jesus. We follow the beliefs and teachings handed down from the apostles. Together we try to live, pray, and work as Jesus taught.

Jesus told his disciples, "You are the light of the world. Your light must shine before others, that they may see your good deeds and glorify your heavenly Father." (Matthew 5:14, 16)

Jesus calls each of us to be a light for all the world to see. When we share our gifts and talents for the good of others, we are a light in the world. When we follow Jesus' example, others can see the goodness of God. They can see the power of God's love in the world.

Celebrating the sacrament of Matrimony at Saint Michael's Russian Catholic Church

Receiving the Eucharist

WE RESPOND

Think about your gifts and talents. They could be things that you enjoy doing or things that you do well. How can you use your gifts and talents for the good of others? Draw one way you can shine for all the world to see.

Circle T if the sentence is true. Circle F if the sentence is false.

1. Catholics live all over the world.

   T   F

2. A Rite is a special way that Catholics celebrate, live, and pray to God.

   T   F

3. Only some Catholics celebrate seven sacraments.

   T   F

4. All Catholics are united with their bishops and the pope.

   T   F

Answer the question.

5. You are a light in the world. What does this mean?

   _____

   _____

   _____

ASSESSMENT

This week, find out about the Catholic Church in another part of the world. Draw a picture or write a paragraph about the language, music, a saint, or a special custom found in that part of the world.

We Respond in Faith

Reflect & Pray

I celebrate, live, and pray my faith by

_____

_____

Finish this prayer.

Heavenly Father, we are united by our belief in Jesus Christ, your Son. Help all members of your Church to

_____

_____

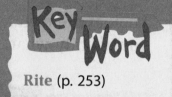

Key Word

Rite (p. 253)

Remember

- The Catholic Church is all over the world.
- Catholics share the same faith.
- Catholics celebrate their faith in different ways.
- We are the light of the world.

OUR CATHOLIC LIFE

One Faith, Many Languages

The Catholic Church shows respect for the languages of its members. The Mass and the sacraments are celebrated in many languages, such as English, French, Spanish, Polish, Armenian, Greek, Ukrainian, Albanian, Romanian, Syrian, Coptic, and Ethiopian. They are also celebrated in many Native American languages.

SHARING FAITH
with My Family

Sharing What I Learned

Look at the pictures below. Use each picture to tell your family what you learned in this chapter.

We Believe Trading Cards

Ask your family to help you design a **Helping the Kingdom Grow** trading card. Attach a photo or draw an image of a family member on the front. Complete the faith facts about this person on the back.

Family Prayer

"May all the peoples praise you, God;
may all the peoples praise you!" (Psalm 67:4)

Helping the Kingdom Grow

Name _____

My favorite time and place to pray is

_____.

My favorite story about Jesus is

_____.

I will learn more about the Catholic Church by

_____.

FOLD ON THIS LINE

Connect to the Catechism
For adult background and reflection, see paragraphs 835, 1203, 1204, and 2105.

We Are God's Holy People

25

Saint Peter

Saint Elizabeth of Hungary

Saint Mary Magdalen

Saint Francis

WE GATHER

✝ **Leader:** Let us sing a song to the saints.

🎵 **Sing a Song to the Saints**

Chorus:
Sing a song to the saints,
   the saints of God the most
   high.
Sing a song to the saints,
   with names like yours
   and mine.

Saint Francis, pray for us.
Saint Cecilia, pray for us.
Saint Peter, pray for us.
Saint Mary Magdalen,
   pray for us.
Sing a song to the saints.

Saint George, pray for us.
Blessed Mary, pray for us.
Saint Thomas, pray for us.
Saint Anastasia, pray for us.
Sing a song to the saints.

Saint Benedict, pray for us.
Saint Margaret, pray for us.
Saint Joseph, pray for us.
Saint Elizabeth, pray for us.
Sing a song to the saints.

☀ What are some ways we remember and honor special people who have lived before us?

211

WE BELIEVE

We belong to the communion of saints.

God is holy. He shares his holiness with us when we are baptized. The word *saint* means "one who is holy." God calls all of us to be saints. Saints are followers of Christ who lived lives of holiness on earth and now share in eternal life with God in heaven.

The saints are examples of holiness. We learn from them how to love God and care for others. Their lives show us how to be true disciples of Jesus.

The Church honors all the saints in heaven in a special way on November 1. We call this day the feast of All Saints. On this day we remember the holy people who have gone before us. We ask them to pray for us always.

Raphael (1483–1570),
The Madonna of the Chair

Edith Catlin Phelps (1875–1961),
Wayside Madonna

The union of the baptized members of the Church on earth with those who are in heaven and in purgatory is called the communion of saints. Through Baptism we are united to Christ and one another. We are united with all members of the Church who are alive on earth, and all who have died and are in heaven or purgatory.

Saints come from all over the world. Who are some saints you know about?

_____

_____

_____

Tell about them.

212

Mary is the greatest of all the saints.

Mary was blessed by God. She was free from original sin from the very first moment of her life. This belief is called the **Immaculate Conception**.

Mary was chosen by God and asked to be the mother of his Son. Mary said, "May it be done to me according to your word" (Luke 1:38). Mary trusted God completely.

Mary loved and cared for Jesus. She listened to his teachings and saw the ways he treated others. She believed in him when others did not. She stayed at the cross as he was dying. She was with the disciples when the Holy Spirit first came to them.

When Mary's work on earth was done, God brought her body and soul to live forever with the risen Christ. This belief is called the **Assumption**.

Mary was Jesus' mother. She is the mother of the Church, too. Jesus loved and honored his mother. The Church loves and honors Mary as well. When we remember Mary, we remember Jesus. We remember that God sent his Son to us.

Mary is an example for all of Jesus' disciples. Mary is the greatest of all the saints. We pray special prayers to honor Mary. The Hail Mary is one of these prayers. In the Hail Mary we praise Mary and ask her to pray for us.

 Talk about ways we can follow Mary's example. Then pray together the Hail Mary found on page 241.

Father John Giuliani,
Hopi Virgin and Child II

Key Words

saints (p. 253)

communion of saints (p. 250)

Immaculate Conception (p. 251)

Assumption (p. 250)

As Catholics...

A *canonized* saint is a person who has been officially named a saint by the Church. The life of this person has been examined by Church leaders. They have decided that the person has lived a life of faith and holiness.

When someone is canonized a saint, his or her name is entered into the worldwide list of saints recognized by the Catholic Church. Each canonized saint has a special feast day.

Is your parish named after a saint? What do you know about him or her?

The Church remembers and honors Mary.

Catholics all over the world honor Mary. We remember how God blessed her. We remember Mary when we celebrate Mass on her feast days.

Another way to honor Mary is by praying the rosary. The rosary combines many prayers. When we pray the rosary, we recall special times in the lives of Mary and Jesus. The mysteries of the rosary recall these special times. We remember a different mystery at the beginning of each decade, or set of ten small beads.

We use rosary beads like this one to say the rosary. Read these directions.

1. Start at the crucifix with the *Sign of the Cross*.

2. Then pray the *Apostles' Creed*.

3. Pray an *Our Father* at every large bead.

4. Pray a *Hail Mary* at every small bead.

5. Pray a *Glory to the Father* after each set of small beads.

6. Pray the *Hail, Holy Queen* to end the rosary.

With a partner discuss why the rosary is a special prayer. Plan when you can pray the rosary.

Joyful Mysteries

The Annunciation

The Visitation

The Nativity

The Presentation

The Finding of the Child Jesus in the Temple

Sorrowful Mysteries

The Agony in the Garden

The Scourging at the Pillar

The Crowning with Thorns

The Carrying of the Cross

The Crucifixion

Glorious Mysteries

The Resurrection

The Ascension

The Coming of the Holy Spirit upon the Apostles

The Assumption of Mary

The Coronation of Mary

Mysteries of Light

Jesus' Baptism in the Jordan

The Miracle at the Wedding at Cana

Jesus Announces the Kingdom of God

The Transfiguration

The Institution of the Eucharist

We can also honor Mary by praying a litany. In a litany for Mary, we call on her by using some of her many titles. After the leader prays each title, we repeat a response.

God calls us to be saints.

The saints answered God's call to lead holy lives. Men, women, and children from every part of the world have become saints. Here are some examples:

- Saint Louise de Marillac was a wife and mother. After her husband died, she began the Daughters of Charity. They served the needs of people who were poor.

Saint Louise de Marillac

- Saint Charles Lwanga lived in Uganda, Africa. He was baptized as an adult. He helped many people in Africa, including those who served in the king's court, to become Christians.

- Saint Joan of Arc was a soldier in France. She tried her best to obey God's will.

- Saint Andrew Nam-Thuong was a mayor of a Vietnamese village. He taught others about the faith.

Saint Andrew Nam-Thuong

- Saint Dominic Savio was a boy who prayed to God everyday. Dominic saw God in the happenings of everyday life. He was always ready to help out a classmate.

God calls you to become a saint, too. How can you become a saint? You can know and live your faith every day. You can learn as much as possible about Jesus and the way he treated others. You can also find out more about the lives of the saints.

God helps each of us to be holy. We are strengthened by prayer. We receive grace from the sacraments. We also get support from our family and our parish. Together we can follow Jesus and grow in holiness.

WE RESPOND

With a partner list people who could be on a "Saints of Our Time" Web site. Give some reasons why they might be included.

_____

_____

_____

_____

_____

Use these terms to complete the sentences.

saints	communion of saints
Immaculate Conception	Assumption

1. The union of all the baptized members of the Church on earth with those who are in heaven and in purgatory is the

_____.

2. The _____ is the belief that, when Mary's work on earth was done, God brought her body and soul to live forever with the risen Christ.

3. The _____ is the belief that Mary was free from original sin from the very first moment of her life.

4. Those who lived a life of holiness and now share in

eternal life with God are _____.

Answer the question.

5. How can you become a saint?

_____

_____

ASSESSMENT

Interview a family member or friend. Ask him or her to name a favorite saint and to tell why. As a class, make a chart to show which saints are favorites and why.

We Respond in Faith

Reflect & Pray

Catholics have many titles for Mary. Each title tells us something special about her. Which title do you think of when you remember Mary?

Write a prayer using this title of Mary.

_____

_____

_____

_____

Key Words

saints (p. 253)
communion of saints
(p. 250)
Immaculate Conception
(p. 251)
Assumption (p. 250)

Remember

- We belong to the communion of saints.
- Mary is the greatest of all the saints.
- The Church remembers and honors Mary.
- God calls us to be saints.

OUR CATHOLIC LIFE

Praying for the Dead

As members of the communion of saints, we pray for all those who have died. We do this at every Mass.

The Church sets aside a special day each year for remembering the dead. This day is November 2, All Souls' Day. On this day we pray for all those who have died, especially during the past year. We pray that they may enjoy eternal life with God forever.

Sharing What I Learned

Look at the pictures below. Use each picture to tell your family what you learned in this chapter.

We Believe Trading Cards

Ask your family to help you design a **Helping the Kingdom Grow** trading card. Attach a photo or draw an image of a family member on the front. Complete the faith facts about this person on the back.

Family of Saints

Look for the names of saints in your neighborhood. Ask your family members to share what they know about each saint.

Helping the Kingdom Grow

FOLD ON THIS LINE

Name _____

My favorite time and place to pray is

_____.

My favorite story about Jesus is

_____.

I will honor Mary and the saints by

_____.

Visit Sadlier's
www.WEBELIEVEweb.com

Connect to the Catechism
For adult background and reflection, see paragraphs 957, 972, 971, and 2013.

WE GATHER

✝ **Leader:** The disciples of Jesus said to him, "Lord, teach us to pray." (Luke 11:1)

We, too, pray by following the teachings of Jesus. Let us pray the Lord's Prayer together.

Our Father, who art in heaven,
(head back, arms raised high)

hallowed be thy name;
(head down, arms crossed on chest)

thy kingdom come;
(right arm stretched out, palm up)

thy will be done on earth
(both arms pointing down to earth)

as it is in heaven.
(raise both arms to heaven)

Give us this day our daily bread;
(cup hands in front)

and forgive us our trespasses
(hold cupped hands up high)

as we forgive those who trespass against us;
(take hands with those on either side)

and lead us not into temptation,
(hold right hand out, palm facing away)

but deliver us from evil.
(bring hand over heart)

Amen.
(bring both arms down to sides, head bowed, palms open)

☀ Name a favorite story. What have you learned from this story?

WE BELIEVE

Jesus used parables to teach about the Kingdom of God.

Jesus wanted to teach the people about God's Kingdom. The people of Jesus' time had heard about the Kingdom of God. Many of them thought God's Kingdom was about power and money. They thought it was like an earthly kingdom.

The kingdom that Jesus taught about was not the kingdom the people expected. Jesus wanted everyone to know that the Kingdom of God is the power of God's love active in the world. To help them understand this, Jesus told the people parables. A **parable** is a short story that uses things from everyday life. Parables are stories with a message.

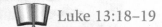 Luke 13:18–19

Jesus described the Kingdom of God with this parable. He said, "What is the kingdom of God like? To what can I compare it? It is like a mustard seed that a person took and planted in the garden. When it was fully grown, it became a large bush and 'the birds of the sky dwelt in its branches.'" (Luke 13:18–19)

Jesus was telling his disciples that, although small, the kingdom would grow. As more people respond to God's love, the Kingdom of God will grow. When we believe in and follow Jesus Christ, we respond to God's love and the kingdom grows.

🧍 Name some signs of God's love active in our world today.

_____

_____

Key Word
parable (p. 252)

Jesus taught that the Kingdom of God will grow.

Jesus taught his disciples that the Kingdom of God is a kingdom of love. God's love was already active among them. Through Jesus' words and actions, the kingdom had begun. The kingdom would grow as more people followed Jesus and believed his message.

The kingdom begins with the good news of Jesus Christ. It continues when we, his disciples, respond to God's love. We show by our words and actions that God's love is active in our lives and in the world. We pray for the time when God's love will rule the world. We pray for the coming of God's Kingdom in its fullness.

Make up a new parable that describes the Kingdom of God. Use things that are familiar to people today. Share your parable by writing or drawing it. Then act it out.

Jesus' miracles were signs of the Kingdom of God.

Jesus did amazing things that only God could do. He calmed the stormy seas, made the blind to see, walked on water, and even changed water into wine. These amazing events were beyond human power. They were **miracles**.

Jesus' miracles showed that he was divine. They were special signs that God's Kingdom was present in him. His miracles helped people to believe that he was the Son of God.

Key Word

miracles (p. 252)

 Matthew 14:22–33

Christ Walking on the Water (Armenian miniature, twelfth-thirteenth century)

One day Jesus' disciples were out in a boat on the sea. Jesus went up to a mountain to pray alone. As night approached "the boat, already a few miles offshore, was being tossed about by the waves, for the wind was against it. During the fourth watch of the night, he came toward them, walking on the sea. When the disciples saw him walking on the sea they were terrified. 'It is a ghost,' they said, and they cried out in fear. At once [Jesus] spoke to them, 'Take courage, it is I; do not be afraid.' Peter said to him in reply, 'Lord, if it is you, command me to come to you on the water.' He said, 'Come.' Peter got out of the boat and began to walk on the water toward Jesus. But when he saw how [strong] the wind was he became frightened; and, beginning to sink, he cried out, 'Lord, save me!' Immediately Jesus stretched out his hand and caught him." (Matthew 14:24–31)

After Jesus and Peter got into the boat the wind stopped. The disciples who were in the boat said, "Truly, you are the Son of God." (Matthew 14:33)

Jesus' walking on water strengthened the faith of his disciples. The first disciples knew Jesus, saw his miracles, and believed.

They told others about Jesus and tried to live as he taught them. By their words and actions, the disciples were witnesses to Jesus.

Witnesses speak and act based upon what they know and believe. We are called to show our faith in Jesus and to be his witnesses.

Write one way you can show others that you have faith in Jesus.

The Kingdom of God grows.

For the past two thousand years, members of the Church have helped one another to be witnesses to Jesus Christ. We can be witnesses by:

- treating people with kindness and respect
- living peacefully with one another
- being fair with all those we meet
- doing what is right even when it is hard
- being faithful members of the Church
- working together for justice and peace.

In the Lord's Prayer we pray for the final coming of God's Kingdom that will take place when Jesus returns in glory. Jesus' coming at the end of time will be a joyful event. It will bring about the fullness of God's Kingdom.

The Church does not pray only for the coming of God's Kingdom. We also ask God the Father to help us to spread the kingdom in our families, schools, and neighborhoods. Everyone in the Church works together so that God's love may be active and present throughout the world.

WE RESPOND

What would you put in a time capsule to show how the Church has spread God's Kingdom? Why?

Review

Grade 3
Chapter 26

Use the words in the box to complete the sentences.

| miracles | kingdom | parable |
| witnesses | mustard seed | |

1. A _____ is a short story that uses things from everyday life.

2. Jesus said that the Kingdom of God is like a

_____.

3. _____ are amazing events that are beyond human power.

4. The Church encourages us to be

_____ to Jesus Christ.

Answer the question.

5. How can I witness to God's Kingdom today?

_____

_____

ASSESSMENT

With your family, find a story in your parish bulletin, diocesan newspaper, or on the Internet that shows Catholics helping to spread God's Kingdom. Write a short report or draw a picture about the story. Tell what people can learn from this story.

224

We Respond in Faith

Reflect & Pray

If I am to spread God's Kingdom, I must be like the good, rich soil. Each day, no matter how hard it is, I will try to witness to God's Kingdom by

_____

_____

Jesus, help me to

_____

_____

Key Words

parable (p. 252)
miracles (p. 252)

Remember

- Jesus used parables to teach about the Kingdom of God.
- Jesus taught that the Kingdom of God will grow.
- Jesus' miracles were signs of the Kingdom of God.
- The Kingdom of God grows.

OUR CATHOLIC LIFE

Tell your story here.

Place your photo here.

SHARING FAITH
with My Family

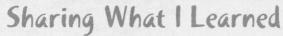

Sharing What I Learned

Look at the pictures below. Use each picture to tell your family what you learned in this chapter.

CLOTHING DRIVE

We Believe Trading Cards

Ask your family to fill out the back of this family trading card together. You might attach a family photo or group drawing on the front. Then collect all your trading cards.

Family Prayer

(Lead your family in this prayer.)

Dear God, help us share our love for one another and share our love for you. Amen.

Helping the Kingdom Grow

FOLD ON THIS LINE

Name _____

Our favorite time and place to pray is

_____.

Our favorite story about Jesus is

_____.

Our family will help the Kingdom of God grow by

_____.

Visit Sadlier's

www.WeBelieveweb.com

Connect to the Catechism
For adult background and reflection, see paragraphs 546, 541, 548, and 2818.

Easter

Advent | Christmas | Ordinary Time | Lent | Three Days | Easter | Ordinary Time

"Blessed are those who have not seen and have believed." (John 20:29)

In the Easter season, we celebrate the Resurrection of Jesus.

WE GATHER

Name three things that you believe about God.

WE BELIEVE

Jesus has risen from the dead! During the Easter season, we celebrate the Resurrection of Jesus, for fifty days! We begin the Easter season on Easter Sunday. It ends fifty days later, on Pentecost Sunday.

The color white is a symbol of light and joy. The priest wears white vestments all during the Easter season. The coverings on the altar are white, also. The entire Easter season is a great celebration of the light, life, and joy of the risen Jesus.

Celebrating the fifty days of Easter strengthens our faith. We show our belief in the risen Jesus.

📖 John 20:19–29

On the night of his Resurrection, Jesus' disciples were hiding in a room. The doors were locked. The risen Jesus suddenly appeared and wished them peace.

One of the apostles, Thomas, was not there that night. The other disciples told him about Jesus. Thomas did not believe them. Thomas wanted to see Jesus for himself. He not only wanted to see Jesus. He wanted to touch Jesus with his own hands!

A week later, the disciples were together again in the locked room. This time Thomas was with them. Suddenly Jesus was there among them. Jesus said to them, "Peace be with you" (John 20:26).

"Then he said to Thomas, 'Put your finger here and see my hands, and bring your hand and put it into my side, and do not be unbelieving, but believe'" (John 20:27).

Thomas fell on his knee before Jesus and said, "My Lord and my God!" (John 20:28)

And Jesus said to him, "Blessed are those who have not seen and have believed" (John 20:29).

We believe in Jesus Christ. We believe in his life, death, and Resurrection. We believe that Jesus brings us new life, now and forever.

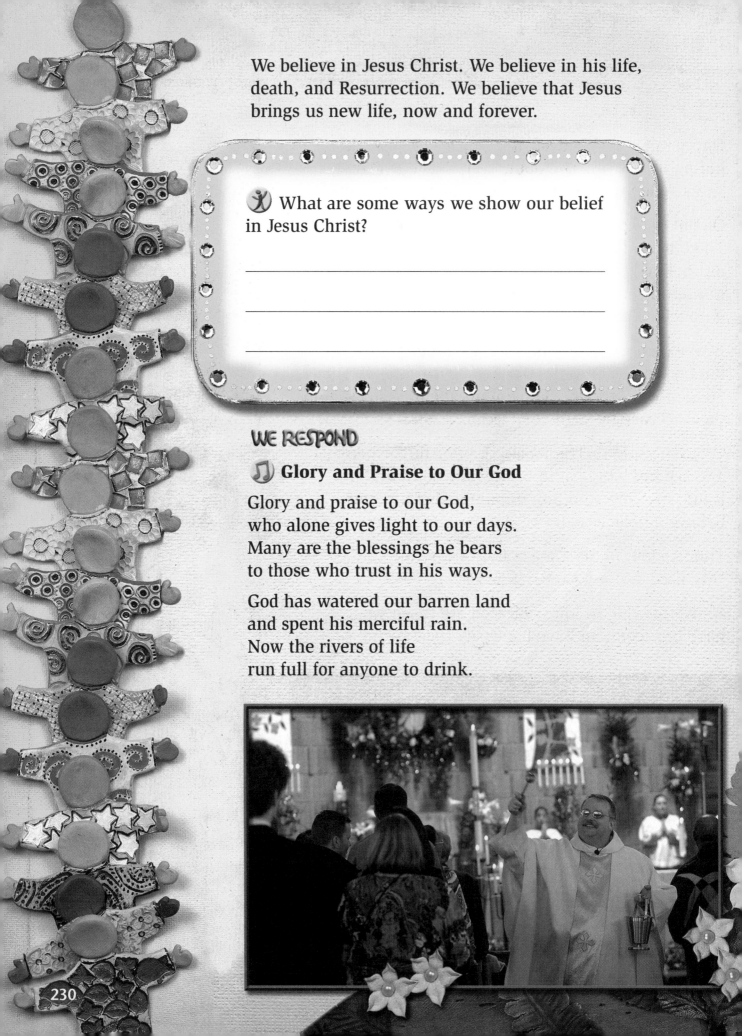

What are some ways we show our belief in Jesus Christ?

_____

_____

_____

WE RESPOND

Glory and Praise to Our God

Glory and praise to our God,
who alone gives light to our days.
Many are the blessings he bears
to those who trust in his ways.

God has watered our barren land
and spent his merciful rain.
Now the rivers of life
run full for anyone to drink.

✝ We Respond in Prayer

Leader: Lord, we believe; increase our faith.

All: Lord, we believe; increase our faith.

Leader: In this Easter season we rejoice in the Resurrection. We ask God to bless us and strengthen our belief.

Reader: So that we can live as your Son, Jesus, calls us to live.

All: Lord, increase our faith.

Reader: So that we can share the good news of Jesus Christ with all we meet.

All: Lord, increase our faith.

Reader: So that we can grow in our love for you.

All: Lord, increase our faith.

EASTER

SHARING FAITH
with My Family

Sharing What I Learned

Look at the pictures below. Use them to tell your family what you learned in this chapter.

An Easter Game

This Easter egg game comes from Europe. Give out dyed hard boiled eggs. Take turns lightly tapping the ends of your egg with one another. If one end cracks, try the other end. If both ends crack, you are out of the game. The egg that stays whole or only cracks on one end is the Alleluia egg!

Easter Prayer of Joy

The Easter season is a time of joy. We celebrate our belief in Jesus' Resurrection. Write a family prayer to express this Easter joy.

_____

_____

_____

_____

Visit Sadlier's
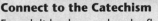
www.WeBelieveweb.com

Connect to the Catechism
For adult background and reflection, see paragraph 644.

Theo's Good News!

"Why won't it ring?" Theo kept staring at the phone.

"We'll learn soon enough," laughed his Uncle Jack. "Be patient, Theo."

Theo's mother was having a baby. Dad had driven her to the hospital earlier that day.

RING!!!!!! RING!!!!!!!!!!!!!!!!

Theo picked up the phone. It was his father. "Theo! It's a girl!"

> "Do not be afraid; for behold, I proclaim to you good news of great joy."
>
> Luke 2:10

Theo couldn't wait to share the good news. "I want to tell everybody," said Theo.

"Before you tell the whole world," laughed his uncle, "help me with this."

Theo helped his uncle hang the "It's a Girl!" banner on the front door.

"Now everybody really will know our good news!" smiled big brother Theo.

Talk About It

• What are some other kinds of good news?

• How do you share good news?

Because *We Believe*

When something wonderful happens we want others to know. At Pentecost the first disciples were filled with the Holy Spirit. They then shared the good news of Jesus with people from different parts of the world. This is how the Church began. We can help the Church continue to grow by sharing our love for Jesus.

How do we show we believe this?

233

We can carry out Jesus' work in the world by sharing his good news with others.

With Your Class

Work with your classmates to make a "*Good News*-paper."

- Give your paper a name.
- Write a story about Jesus' good news.

"The Christian family has an evangelizing and missionary task."

(Catechism of the Catholic Church, 2205)

With Your Family

Read page 233 together. Talk about ways we share good news with others.

Take a look at your family. What "good news" do you see?

- What is something our family does well together?
- How did someone in our family help me today?
- How has our family helped others?

Pray Together

Loving Jesus,

Our family and parish have been blessed with your good news.

Amen.

SHARING FAITH
in Class and at Home

Look at the pictures. Circle the signs of God's love.

Talk About It

Look at what you circled. Why are these signs of God's love?

Because *We Believe*

A sacrament is a special sign given to us by Jesus. Through the sacraments we receive and share in God's own life and love. The Church celebrates seven sacraments. The seven sacraments are Baptism, Confirmation, Eucharist, Reconciliation, Anointing of the Sick, Matrimony, and Holy Orders.

How do we show we believe this?

Christ the King PARISH Clothing Drive

"For you are great and do wondrous deeds; and you alone are God."

Psalm 86:10

We can be signs of God's love by what we say and do.

With Your Class

Work in small groups and discuss:

- things you can do to make new classmates feel welcome

- ideas for making your classroom a more forgiving place

- ways that your class can reach out to people in need in your community.

With Your Family

Read page 235 together. Talk about the signs of God's love that are around us. Answer these questions.

- How does your family offer forgiveness to one another?

- How does your family show love for one another?

- How does your family help people outside of your home?

"The family should live in such a way that its members learn to care and take responsibility for the young, the old, the sick, the handicapped, and the poor."

(Catechism of the Catholic Church, 2208)

Pray Together

"Teach me, LORD, your way
that I may walk in your truth. . . .
I will praise you with
all my heart,
glorify your name forever,
Lord my God.
Your love for me is great."

Psalm 86:11–13

NOW WHAT?
Bring this page back to Class ▢   Keep this page at Home ▢

SHARING FAITH
in Class and at Home

A Good Example

Ben and Will could not believe their luck. Ben's mom had gotten tickets for the soccer game. Ben wanted to be just like Michael Wilson, the star soccer player.

Suddenly Michael Wilson was right in front of Ben and Will! The crowd moved toward the soccer star. Then a small frightened voice called, "Help!" The crowd was pushing a young child! In a split second, Michael Wilson raced to the child's side. He quickly picked her up until her parents were able to get to her.

Ben now knew another reason why he wanted to be just like Michael Wilson.

What Do You Think?

• How is Michael Wilson a good example?

• Why did Ben want to be like Michael?

Because *We Believe*

Saints are examples, too. They are followers of Jesus who lived lives of holiness on earth and now share eternal life with God. Saints show us how to be disciples of Jesus.

Disciples of Jesus Christ are *witnesses* to their faith. We are witnesses when we treat others with kindness and respect. We are witnesses when we live peacefully and fairly with others. We are witnesses when we do what is right even when it is hard.

How do we show we believe this?

"For those who are led by the Spirit of God are children of God."

Romans 8:14

All of us can be witnesses by sharing our belief in Jesus through our words and actions.

With Your Class

Saints show us how to be disciples of Jesus. Name a saint whom you admire.

• How does his or her life serve as a witness to the faith?

• How do you want to be like him or her?

A march for peace

"Becoming a disciple of Jesus means accepting the invitation to belong to *God's family*, to live in conformity with His way of life."

(Catechism of the Catholic Church, 2233)

With Your Family

Read page 237. Talk about what it means to be a witness to faith in Jesus Christ.

Use newspapers, magazines, or the Internet to find pictures and stories of people who are witnesses to faith in Jesus through their words and actions. Share these stories with your family. List ways that your family can be witnesses to faith in Jesus.

Pray Together

Mary is our greatest example of witness.
Pray the Hail Mary together.

NOW WHAT? Bring this page back to class ☐   Keep this page at home ☐

238

Assessment

Grade 3
Unit 4

Fill in the circle beside the correct answer.

1. Through _____ each if us is called to share the good news of Jesus.

   ○ the pope and   ○ justice and peace   ○ the sacrament
     bishops   of Baptism

2. Working with other Christians to bring together all baptized people is called _____.

   ○ ecumenism   ○ a mosaic   ○ a covenant

3. Catholics who celebrate, live, and pray according to the Eastern Rites and Latin Rite all share in the same _____.

   ○ sacraments   ○ customs   ○ languages

4. When we say that Mary was free from original sin from the first moment of her life, we are speaking of her _____.

   ○ Annunciation   ○ Assumption   ○ Immaculate
                                                    Conception

5. In a parable Jesus explained that people who care too much about owning things are like _____.

   ○ the good soil   ○ the soil filled   ○ the mustard seed
                          with thorns

Use your own words to complete these sentences.

6. The communion of saints is _____

   _____.

7. I can answer Jesus' call to be a light for all the world by _____

   _____.

239

Using the clues in ( ) for help, unscramble the letters to make words. Write the letters in the spaces and circles below.

1. (event in Mary's life) SNAOSIUTMP

◯__ __ __◯__ __◯__ __

2. (agreement) TNANCEOV

◯__ __◯__ __ __ __

3. (people who lived holy lives) STSANI

◯__ __ __ __ __

4. (story) BLAPARE

__ __◯__ __◯__

Now write the circled letters here.

◯◯◯◯◯◯◯◯

Unscramble the circled letters to find the word that finishes this sentence:

Amazing events beyond human power are called

__ __ __ __ __ __ __ __.

Now use each of the five unscrambled words in a sentence.

Prayers and Practices

Sign of the Cross

In the name of the Father, and of the Son,
and of the Holy Spirit. Amen.

Our Father

Our Father, who art in heaven,
hallowed be thy name;
thy kingdom come;
thy will be done on earth
    as it is in heaven.
Give us this day our daily bread;
and forgive us our trespasses
as we forgive those
    who trespass against us;
and lead us not into temptation,
but deliver us from evil. Amen.

Glory to the Father

Glory to the Father, and to the Son,
    and to the Holy Spirit:
as it was in the beginning,
    is now, and will be forever. Amen.

Hail Mary

Hail Mary, full of grace,
the Lord is with you!
Blessed are you among women,
and blessed is the fruit
    of your womb, Jesus.
Holy Mary, Mother of God,
pray for us sinners,
now and at the hour of our death.
Amen.

Act of Contrition

My God,
I am sorry for my sins with all my heart.
In choosing to do wrong
and failing to do good,
I have sinned against you
whom I should love above all things.
I firmly intend, with your help,
to do penance,
to sin no more,
and to avoid whatever leads me to sin.
Our Savior Jesus Christ
suffered and died for us.
In his name, my God, have mercy.

• contrition •

• confession •

• penance •

• absolution •

Morning Offering

My God, I offer you this day
all that I think and do and say,
uniting it with what was done
on earth, by Jesus Christ, your Son.

Evening Prayer

Dear God, before I sleep
I want to thank you for this day
so full of your kindness and your joy.
I close my eyes to rest
safe in your loving care.

Grace Before Meals

Bless † us, O Lord,
   and these your gifts,
which we are about to receive
   from your goodness.
Through Christ our Lord. Amen.

Grace After Meals

We give you thanks, almighty God,
for these and all your gifts
which we have received through
Christ our Lord. Amen.

Stations of the Cross

In the stations we follow in the footsteps of Jesus during his passion and death on the cross.

Jesus is condemned to die.

Jesus takes up his cross.

Jesus falls the first time.

Jesus meets his mother.

Simon helps Jesus carry his cross.

Veronica wipes the face of Jesus.

Jesus falls the second time.

Jesus meets the women of Jerusalem.

Jesus falls the third time.

Jesus is stripped of his garments.

Jesus is nailed to the cross.

Jesus dies on the cross.

Jesus is taken down from the cross.

Jesus is laid in the tomb.

Apostles' Creed

I believe in God, the Father almighty,
 creator of heaven and earth.

I believe in Jesus Christ,
 his only Son, our Lord.
He was conceived by the power
 of the Holy Spirit
 and born of the Virgin Mary.
He suffered under Pontius Pilate,
 was crucified, died, and was buried.
He descended to the dead.
On the third day he rose again.
He ascended into heaven,
 and is seated at the right hand
 of the Father.
He will come again to judge
 the living and the dead.

I believe in the Holy Spirit,
 the holy catholic Church,
 the communion of saints,
 the forgiveness of sins,
 the resurrection of the body,
 and the life everlasting.
Amen.

The Rosary

A rosary is made up of groups of beads arranged in a circle. It begins with a cross followed by one large bead and three small ones. The next large bead (just before the medal) begins the first "decade." Each decade consists of one large bead followed by ten smaller beads.

Begin the rosary with the Sign of the Cross. Recite the Apostles' Creed. Then pray one Our Father, three Hail Marys, and one Glory to the Father.

To pray each decade, say an Our Father on the large bead and a Hail Mary on each of the ten smaller beads. Close each decade by praying the Glory to the Father. Pray the Hail, Holy Queen as the last prayer of the rosary.

The mysteries of the rosary are special events in the lives of Jesus and Mary. As you pray each decade, think of the appropriate Joyful Mystery, Sorrowful Mystery, Glorious Mystery, or Mystery of Light.

The Five Joyful Mysteries

1. The Annunciation
2. The Visitation
3. The Birth of Jesus
4. The Presentation of Jesus in the Temple
5. The Finding of Jesus in the Temple

The Five Sorrowful Mysteries

1. The Agony in the Garden
2. The Scourging at the Pillar
3. The Crowning with Thorns
4. The Carrying of the Cross
5. The Crucifixion and Death of Jesus

The Five Glorious Mysteries

1. The Resurrection
2. The Ascension
3. The Coming of the Holy Spirit upon the Apostles
4. The Assumption of Mary into Heaven
5. The Coronation of Mary in Heaven

The Five Mysteries of Light

1. Jesus' Baptism in the Jordan
2. The Miracle at the Wedding at Cana
3. Jesus Announces the Kingdom of God
4. The Transfiguration
5. The Institution of the Eucharist

Hail, Holy Queen

Hail, holy Queen, mother of mercy,
hail, our life, our sweetness, and our hope.
To you we cry, the children of Eve;
to you we send up our sighs,
mourning and weeping in this land of exile.
Turn, then, most gracious advocate,
your eyes of mercy toward us;
lead us home at last and show us
the blessed fruit of your womb, Jesus:
O clement, O loving, O sweet Virgin Mary.

Prayer for My Vocation

Dear God,
You have a great and loving plan
for our world and for me.
I wish to share in that plan fully,
faithfully, and joyfully.

Help me to understand what it
is you wish me to do with my life.
Help me to be attentive to the signs
that you give me about preparing for
the future.

And once I have heard and understood
your call, give me the strength
and the grace to follow it
with generosity and love.
Amen.

Holy Water

A holy water font containing blessed water is placed near the door of the church. When we enter the church, we put our fingers into the holy water and then make the sign of the cross. The water reminds us of our Baptism, and the prayer we say expresses our belief in the Blessed Trinity. Many Catholic families also have holy water in their homes.

Holy Places

We treat places of prayer (churches, synagogues, temples, and mosques) with reverence. In our Catholic churches, we genuflect toward the tabernacle as we enter our pew. Genuflecting (touching our right knee to the floor) is a sign of our reverence for Jesus Christ, who is really present in the Blessed Sacrament.

Visits to the Blessed Sacrament

Before Mass on Sundays or at other special times, take a few minutes to visit Jesus, present in the Blessed Sacrament. After you have taken your place in church, kneel or sit quietly. Be very still. Talk to Jesus about your needs and your hopes. Thank Jesus for his great love. Remember to pray for your family and your parish, especially anyone who is sick or in need.

Prayer Before the Blessed Sacrament

Jesus,
you are God-with-us,
especially in this sacrament
of the Eucharist.
You love me as I am
and help me grow.

Come and be with me
in all my joys and sorrows.
Help me share your peace and love
with everyone I meet.
I ask in your name. Amen.

The Seven Sacraments

The Sacraments of Christian Initiation
Baptism
Confirmation
Eucharist

The Sacraments of Healing
Penance and Reconciliation
Anointing of the Sick

The Sacraments at the Service of Communion
Holy Orders
Matrimony

The Ten Commandments

1. I am the LORD your God: you shall not have strange gods before me.

2. You shall not take the name of the LORD your God in vain.

3. Remember to keep holy the LORD's Day.

4. Honor your father and your mother.

5. You shall not kill.

6. You shall not commit adultery.

7. You shall not steal.

8. You shall not bear false witness against your neighbor.

9. You shall not covet your neighbor's wife.

10. You shall not covet your neighbor's goods.

Glossary

Acts of the Apostles (page 52)
book in the Bible that tells the story of the work of the apostles in the early Church

apostle (page 23)
one who is sent

Apostles' Creed (page 85)
Christian statement of beliefs based on the teachings of Jesus Christ and the faith of the apostles

Ascension (page 44)
Jesus' returning to the Father in heaven

assembly (page 142)
people gathered to worship in the name of Jesus Christ

Assumption (page 213)
the belief that, when Mary's work on earth was done, God brought her body and soul to live forever with the risen Christ

Bible (page 28)
collection of books about God's love for us and our call to live as God's people

bishops (page 77)
the successors of the apostles who lead the Church

Blessed Trinity (page 20)
the three Persons in one God: God the Father, God the Son, and God the Holy Spirit

Christians (page 46)
baptized people, followers of Jesus Christ

Church (page 46)
community of people who are baptized and follow Jesus Christ

communion of saints (page 212)
the union of the baptized members of the Church on earth with those who are in heaven and in purgatory

Concluding Rites (page 151)
the last part of the Mass that remind us to continue praising and serving God each day

conscience (page 158)
God's gift that helps us know right from wrong

covenant (page 197)
an agreement between God and his people

crucified (page 30)
nailed to a cross

deacon (page 101)
a man who is not a priest but has received the sacrament of Holy Orders and serves the Church by preaching, baptizing, and assisting the bishop and priests

dioceses (page 77)
local areas of the Church led by bishops

disciples (page 22)
those who follow Jesus

ecumenism (page 198)
work toward Christian unity

eternal life (page 166)
living forever with God in the happiness of heaven

Eucharist (page 140)
the sacrament of Jesus' Body and Blood

faith (page 30)
a gift from God that helps us to believe and trust in him

funeral Mass (page 167)
a special Mass at which we thank God for the life of a person who has died

gospel (page 53)
good news that we are saved by Jesus Christ, the Son of God

grace (page 132)
our share in God's life and love

heaven (page 38)
life with God forever

Immaculate Conception (page 213)
the belief that Mary was free from original sin from the very first moment of her life

Incarnation (page 20)
the truth that God the Son became man

Introductory Rites (page 148)
the first part of the Mass in which we become one as we prepare to listen to God's word and to celebrate the Eucharist

justice (page 87)
treating everyone fairly and with respect

Kingdom of God (page 28)
the power of God's love active in the world

last judgment (page 38)
Jesus Christ coming at the end of time to judge all people

laypeople (page 108)
baptized members of the Church who share in the mission to bring the good news of Christ to the world

liturgy (page 93)
the official public prayer of the Church

Liturgy of the Eucharist (page 150)
the part of the Mass when the bread and wine become the Body and Blood of Christ, which we receive in Holy Communion

Liturgy of the Word (page 148)
the part of the Mass when we listen and respond to God's word

marks of the Church (page 78)
four characteristics that describe the Church: The Church is one, holy, catholic, and apostolic.

martyrs (page 54)
people who die for their faith

Mass (page 141)
celebration of the Eucharist

miracles (page 222)
amazing events that are beyond human power

mission (page 44)
special job

oil of the sick (page 165)
holy oil that has been blessed by a bishop for use in the Anointing of the Sick

original sin (page 133)
the first sin committed by the first human beings

parable (page 220)
a short story that uses things from everyday life

parish (page 100)
community of believers who worship and work together

Passover (page 140)
the Jewish feast celebrating freedom from slavery in Egypt

pastor (page 101)
the priest who leads the parish in worship, prayer, and teaching

Pentecost (page 45)
the day the Holy Spirit came upon the apostles

pilgrimages (page 95)
prayer-journeys to holy places

pope (page 77)
the bishop of Rome, who leads the whole Catholic Church

prayer (page 92)
listening and talking to God

prophet (page 22)
someone called by God to speak to the people

public ministry (page 22)
Jesus' work among the people

repent (page 22)
to turn away from sin and to ask God for help to live a good life

Resurrection (page 31)
Jesus' being raised from the dead

Rite (page 205)
a special way that Catholics celebrate, live, and pray to God

sacrament (page 132)
special sign given to us by Jesus through which we share in God's life and love

sacraments of Christian initiation (page 133)
the sacraments of Baptism, Confirmation, and Eucharist

sacrifice (page 141)
a gift offered to God by a priest in the name of all the people

saints (page 212)
followers of Christ who lived lives of holiness on earth and now share in eternal life with God in heaven

second coming (page 37)
Jesus' coming at the end of time

sin (page 156)
a thought, word, or action that is against God's law

synagogue (page 92)
the gathering place where Jewish people pray and learn about God

vocation (page 108)
God's call to serve him in a certain way

vows (page 110)
promises to God

Index

The following is a list of topics that appear in the pupil's text.
Boldface indicates an entire chapter or section.